SCULPTING IN STONE

THE BASICS OF SCULPTURE

SCULPTING IN STONE

John Valentine

A&C Black

First published in Great Britain in 2007
A & C Black Publishers Limited
38 Soho Square
London W1D 3HB
www.acblack.com

ISBN 13: 978-07136-7658-2

CIP Catalogue records for this book are available from the British Library and the US Library of Congress.

Book design by Penny & Tony Mills
Cover design by Sutchinda Rangsi Thompson
Cover images (front): Detail from carved panel by Judith Tucker, and sequence from sculpting an abstract piece
Cover image (back): *Be With Me* by Bernard McGuigan.

Printed and bound in China

This book is produced using paper that is made from wood grown in managed, sustainable forests. It is natural, renewable and recyclable. The logging and manufacturing processes conform to the environmental regulations of the country of origin.

CONTENTS

ACKNOWLEDGEMENTS   7

PREFACE   9

1. AN INTRODUCTION TO THE GEOLOGY OF CARVING STONES   11

   • Plate tectonics   • Igneous, sedimentary and metamorphic rocks

   • Geology from a carver's perspective

2. THE STONE INDUSTRY   21

   • Stone quarries and yards   • Marble and slate yards   • Carvers and masons

3. GETTING STARTED – equipment   27

   • A place to work   • Some tools   • Choosing a stone

4. GETTING STARTED – techniques   33

   • Forming a chamfer   • Forming a rebate

Project 1 **A CELTIC KNOT PATTERN**   39

Project 2 **CARVING AN INSCRIPTION**   49

5. TOOLS AND TECHNIQUES FOR 3D WORK   55

   • Tools for larger work   • Making a flat surface   • Making a curved edge

Project 3 **AN IN-THE-ROUND (3D) CARVING**   63

Project 4 **A MORE FORMAL 3D CARVING**   71

6. MENDING AND HANGING   79

   • Mending a broken corner   • Filling a flush   • Hanging

GLOSSARY   87

RESOURCES   88

GALLERY   90

INDEX   96

ACKNOWLEDGEMENTS

Thanks go to the following:

Ambrose Hearne for advice on geology.

Martin Shawlcross for advice on photography.

Susannah Lydon of the Earth Science Education Unit, Keele University, for advice and photographs.

Albion Stone Quarries Ltd for photographs.

Johnson Wellfield Quarries Ltd for photographs.

Dean and Chapter for images of Southwell Minster.

Fergus Wessel for photographs of his lettering.

Robin Golden-Hann for photographs of his work.

Bernard McGuigan for photographs of his work.

Sophie and Sir Alan Bowness of the Hepworth Estate.

Claudia Schmid from Tate images.

Roger Francis of Francis, Buchanan Ltd for photographs and stone supply.

Shaun Wolff of Wolff Stone Ltd for photographs and stone supply.

Richard Joplin of Alec Tiranti Ltd for photographs.

Judith Tucker and Guy Levett for permission to reproduce photographs of their carvings.

Contact details for artists featured in the book

Judith Tucker
End Cottage, Welford Road
Long Marston CV37 8RG
Tel: 07971 489449
heyjude@btopenworld.com

Robin Golden-Hann
Project Workshops, Lains Farm
Quarley, Nr Andover
Hampshire, SP11 8PX
Tel: 01722 503 832
www.claystone.co.uk
robin@golden-hann.co.uk

Fergus Wessel
Heather Lodge, Upper Milton
Milton-under-Wychwood OX7 6EZ
Tel: 07779 294673
info@stoneletters.com

Guy Levett
c/o CWO Ltd
Terminus Works, Chichester,
PO19 8TX

Bernard McGuigan
The Annexe
1(B) Lady Margaret Road
London NW5 2NE
Tel: 020 7419 4929
www.bernard-mcguigan.co.uk
bernardmcguigan@yahoo.co.uk

(Opposite) A medieval (14th century) style beast by Robin Golden-Hann. Carved for Salisbury Cathedral, and installed on the north side of the nave.

PREFACE

Stone, more than any other medium, connects us with our past. It is the pre-eminent medium of creative record. Its strength and durability, together with its ability to accept detailed shaping, has provided us with images and messages since antiquity. Stone has been carved throughout history, using the same stone types, the same techniques and similar tools. Its longevity means that it is sometimes impossible to even guess the age of a carving by studying its condition.

Many cultures have carved or shaped stone. The ancient Egyptians carved alabaster and other soft stones but they did not have tools hard enough to cut the granites also found in that country. Instead they rubbed or abraded them, laboriously creating the forms that are seen in museums across the world, unchanged by the passage of millennia. In India many limestones, sandstones and marbles continue to be carved, as they are in China. The carvers often sit cross-legged, sometimes in groups, using an adze or small pick rather than a hammer and chisel. There may be a forge nearby where the tools can be frequently re-tempered and sharpened, and apprentices keep the carvers supplied with fresh equipment.

This book concentrates on the European tradition, which evolved from the techniques used to carve the fine, not very hard, marbles and limestones found in southern and western Europe. The most famous stones of Western antiquity are the white marble of Classical Athens, called Pentelikon, and the similar marble of ancient Rome, still available from the quarries at Carrara. These and other fine stones were used lavishly throughout the Roman Empire for construction and for carving and sculpture. The masons and carvers who shaped them worked standing up, with the stone, if too small to be floor-standing, on a bench at about waist height. They used hammers and mallets of metal and wood, and chisels very similar to those we use today. They created buildings and sculptures for religious, secular and political purposes. In antiquity and the subsequent centuries, no particular role has predominated: a brief knowledge of any European city with a tradition of stone buildings and carving will reveal secular and sacred examples equally well made, equally designed to last.

So whoever picks up a chisel and cuts into a stone block is entering a tradition measured in millennia. At the same time, he or she is creating an object that, in its turn, may remain recognisable for centuries. Stone offers not only a link with the past but also a way to reach into the future. Today, working in stone can offer the satisfaction of creation by hand. There is a steady slowness, a rhythm, to the process, and less need for articulate thought, perhaps contrasting with the way in which many of us spend our working lives: as an artistic medium stone provides a way of transforming an imaginary form into a real one, an idea into an object.

As with all creative activities, the medium and the message both have a role to play in the success of the finished piece. Like any medium, stone imposes limits on what can be made, but it also contributes ideas and possibilities of form, texture and (perhaps less often) colour. But some hands-on experience and a working knowledge of technique are required to understand what those limits and possibilities are. This book is about craft

The limestone carvings in the Chapter House at Southwell Minster were made before 1300.

rather than art, about the practicalities of stone as a medium. The techniques outlined can be applied to any project, at any level of detail that lies in your imagination. The message is up to you.

This book concentrates on four worked projects, and three practical exercises. The first practical exercise (Chapter 4) is designed to give you some initial experience in using carving tools and to develop enough control to cut stone in a straight line. The first worked project (Project 1) shows the process of decorative relief carving using a simple Celtic knot pattern as an example; the second (Project 2) demonstrates the techniques of carving an inscription. Two more practical exercises (Chapter 5) demonstrate some essential sculptural techniques to make curved surfaces.

The third and fourth worked projects illustrate some of the processes of making three-dimensional sculptures. The third project (Project 3) is a free carving, designed to allow you to enjoy the process of carving stone without worrying too much about exact lines and depths, whereas the fourth (Project 4) demands a bit more accuracy, as might be needed for a commissioned piece.

All four projects should result in a finished piece but the exercises are not designed to be kept. The projects are simple in design, and are not technically difficult and do not require great drawing skill. As you gain confidence you may want to increase their complexity or the degree of surface decoration; some examples of more complex work are also shown through the book.

In addition, there are short chapters on the stone industry, the geology of carving stones, and practical details such as choosing stone, repairs, and a description of the hand tools available to carvers.

The exercises and projects described in Chapter 5, and Projects 3 and 4 use limestone. Sandstone is used in Chapter 4, and slate in Project 2. This reflects the popularity of limestone among stone carvers: it is widely available and doesn't have the health risks associated with sandstone, which is made up of quartz grains that should not be inhaled. However, if you live in a sandstone area and don't mind wearing a dust mask, all the limestone exercises and projects can be done in sandstone.

The letter carving project in Project 2 has been worked in slate (a dust mask should also be worn when working with slate), and it would be a good idea to use slate or marble for this project, to get an idea of the accuracy and precision that can be obtained with these stones. But fine limestone or sandstone can be used for this work too, if slate and marble are difficult to obtain. The book does not discuss carving in granite because it is very hard and slow to carve by hand.

As with wood, not all stone is suitable, but good carving stone is widely available and not expensive in small blocks. A set of tools is not costly and will last a lifetime. A mason's bench is made from a few builder's blocks, a paving slab and a bit of old carpet. After that, all you need is eye protection, a dust mask if you are using slate or sandstone, a covered space that can get a bit dusty, and a willingness to try carving in stone for yourself.

CHAPTER 1

AN INTRODUCTION TO THE GEOLOGY OF CARVING STONES

This short chapter has two purposes. The first is to give some idea of the kind of events that took place, and the enormous timescale over which they occurred, that resulted in the block of carving stone that will soon be resting on your work bench. Along the way, the chapter will also relate the geological classification of rocks to the names of the stones that you may encounter as a carver. The second purpose is to give some advice about choosing stone.

A note on the word 'stone'. To a geologist, 'stone' and 'rock' are virtually synonymous. For carvers, 'stone' means any piece of rock that can be controllably shaped. The industry often uses 'stone' to mean building stone, usually limestone or sandstone, as distinct from marble or slate. This book will use the word 'stone' predominantly to mean carveable sandstone or limestone — where marble and slate are included in the definition, they are named.

PLATE TECTONICS

Geologists (or earth scientists) think that the Earth is about 4600 million years old, and that its surface has been moving around for the last 3000 million years. It was not until the mid-1960s that the idea of plate tectonics, or continental drift, was established to explain this surface movement, and the concept is now central to the whole field of Earth science. The movements have been huge. Some 500 million years ago southern Britain was near the Antarctic Circle. It drifted north and reached its present latitude about 50 million years ago, spending most of the intervening time in the tropics. This journey helps to explain Britain's rock and fossil diversity that attracted the attention of the pioneer geologists of the late 18th and early 19th centuries.

The Earth's outer surface, or crust, is made up of tectonic plates, about 62 miles (100km) thick though thinner (6–9 miles/10–15km) under the oceans, which move at between 3 and 10cm (1–4in.) each year due to convection within the mantle. There are seven large plates and several smaller ones. The boundaries between these plates are areas of intense disturbance. Where plates are moving apart new molten material — lava — rises rapidly to the surface. Under the seas, the lava produces a new ocean floor, contributing to sea floor spreading. Over time this causes old oceans to disappear and new ones appear, and two continents on either side of a vanished ocean may then collide, as happened at the Himalayas. Where plates are forced beneath another, deep ocean trenches are formed, called subduction zones. At these zones existing rocks descend back into the mantle, and are folded or melted, perhaps to reappear millions of years later in a new form.

IGNEOUS ROCKS

Below the tectonic plates is the Earth's mantle, which is a thick shell of dense rock that surrounds the liquid metallic outer core, and extends about 2900km below the surface at very great temperatures and pressures. Partial melting of the mantle results in the formation of liquid magma, which is less dense than the surrounding mantle and rises into the Earth's crust, where it arrives at or near the surface as lava and ejecta. All rocks that derive directly from magma are called igneous rocks. Some may have arrived very quickly, like volcanic lava, which cool at the Earth's surface to form basalt. Other rocks may have risen more slowly, and cooled and solidified in the crust over very long periods, and may have remained covered until the overlying rocks weathered away. Granites are examples of such rocks. They have cooled so slowly that large crystals of their component minerals (primarily quartz, feldspar and mica) have been able to grow, giving the characteristic grainy appearance.

SEDIMENTARY ROCKS

Sandstones and limestones are both sedimentary rocks. The origins of sandstone are easier to describe, although, as always with geology, the timescales are enormous. If granite and the igneous rocks have their source in molten magma from the Earth's mantle, sandstone originates in the weathering of those rocks: chemical weathering from carbon dioxide and acids from decaying vegetation, and physical erosion such as the effects of freezing, flowing water and wind.

Of the three minerals that make up most igneous rocks, the hardest of these (and often the most abundant) is quartz, which chemically is silica (SiO_2). Over millions of years of erosion and weathering the other minerals dissolve or wash away, leaving the quartz exposed to break up into small particles of silica, or sand. These sand grains accumulate to form sandbanks if deposited by rivers, or sand-dunes if deposited by winds in desert conditions. They may be made of coarse grains or grits if they are deposited relatively close to the original quartz, or fine sand if they have travelled further or for longer. Sometimes beds may be several metres thick; elsewhere, perhaps where a river has broken its banks, the beds may have thin laminations, useful to us for paving and other thin stone purposes. This process is called the deposition stage of sandstone creation.

The sandbanks or dunes do not become hard until the compaction stage has taken place. The sand deposits are buried and compressed under many metres of overlying rock for many thousands of years, and the pores between the sand grains are filled with clays or limes, or perhaps crystalline silica or iron oxides, carried in solution or suspension in the groundwater. This natural cement binds adjacent grains together to form stone; the usefulness of sandstone depends on the strength of this natural cement as well as the effectiveness of the compression. The photograph shows sandstone under a microscope showing the quartz grains. The grains are still visible when seen through an ordinary magnifying glass.

Limestone has little in common with sandstone, except that its constituent parts have also been deposited over a very long period and then compressed to form rock. It is not made of grains of quartz but of calcium carbonate ($CaCO_3$) — useful limestones are at least 85 per cent calcium carbonate.

There are two main ways in which limestone may be formed; either organically or chemically, although in practice many stones are a mixture of both. Many limestones with organic origins are formed from the broken and decayed fragments of mollusc shells laid down in shallow tropical seas, although there are also a few freshwater limestones; other rare limestones are formed from sea lilies, corals or other fossils.

Offcuts: a small sandstone block to the left, three limestone blocks in the centre with an Italian marble panel beneath, and two slate blocks to the right.

As with sandstone, this deposition stage may last for millions of years and can be influenced by the action of waves and currents. It is followed by a compaction stage, during which most of the mollusc shells are broken into tiny fragments. Some of the calcium carbonate from the shells may be dissolved and then re-deposited — like limescale in a kettle — to act as a cement between the fragments. It is surprising that despite the pressure and the passage of time, some shells remain intact or in large pieces. These are interesting to geologists and biologists, but very shelly stones are not useful to the builder, because the shells weather more slowly than the surrounding calcium carbonate, and eventually will protrude from the cut face of the stone. Shelly stones are not much good for the carver either, because of the shells' brittleness.

A photograph of sandstone under a microscope showing the quartz grains. Photo © Earth Science Education Unit.

The grains are still visible when seen through an ordinary magnifying glass. Photo © Earth Science Education Unit.

Most carving limestones are oolitic stones, which are made predominantly from chemically-formed calcium carbonate. Oolites are tiny balls that in some stones are perhaps half a millimetre in diameter but in others are invisible to the naked eye. These are formed when calcium carbonate precipitates round tiny grains of shell (or perhaps sand). Dissolved calcium carbonate crystallises between oolites to act as cement, and following compression over many years hard and uniform stone is formed. Many oolitic stones also contain some shell fragments — the best carving stones have very few or very small fragments. The photograph shows oolitic limestone under a microscope, with the oolites clearly visible.

Readers in the Unites States may know that the town of Oolitic, Indiana, claims to be 'the limestone capital of the world'. In 1896 the citizens applied for the name of Limestone, but that had already been taken, so they settled for Oolitic, and the name was incorporated in 1901. Some very large quarries north of the town have been in continuous operation since the 1830s. A major visitor attraction is Empire Hole, the quarry (now defunct) that supplied stone for the Empire State Building in New York.

Limestone deposits can be many tens of metres deep and contain many different beds deposited in different eras. These beds vary in quality from the shelliest, most sandy, crumbly stone to the finest stone. Bed thicknesses — which dictate the maximum size of available blocks — also vary from less than a metre to sometimes three or four metres. Sometimes good stone is found fairly near the surface; in other places a lot of useless material has to be removed first. The working face of any limestone quarry will tell its own unique story — different

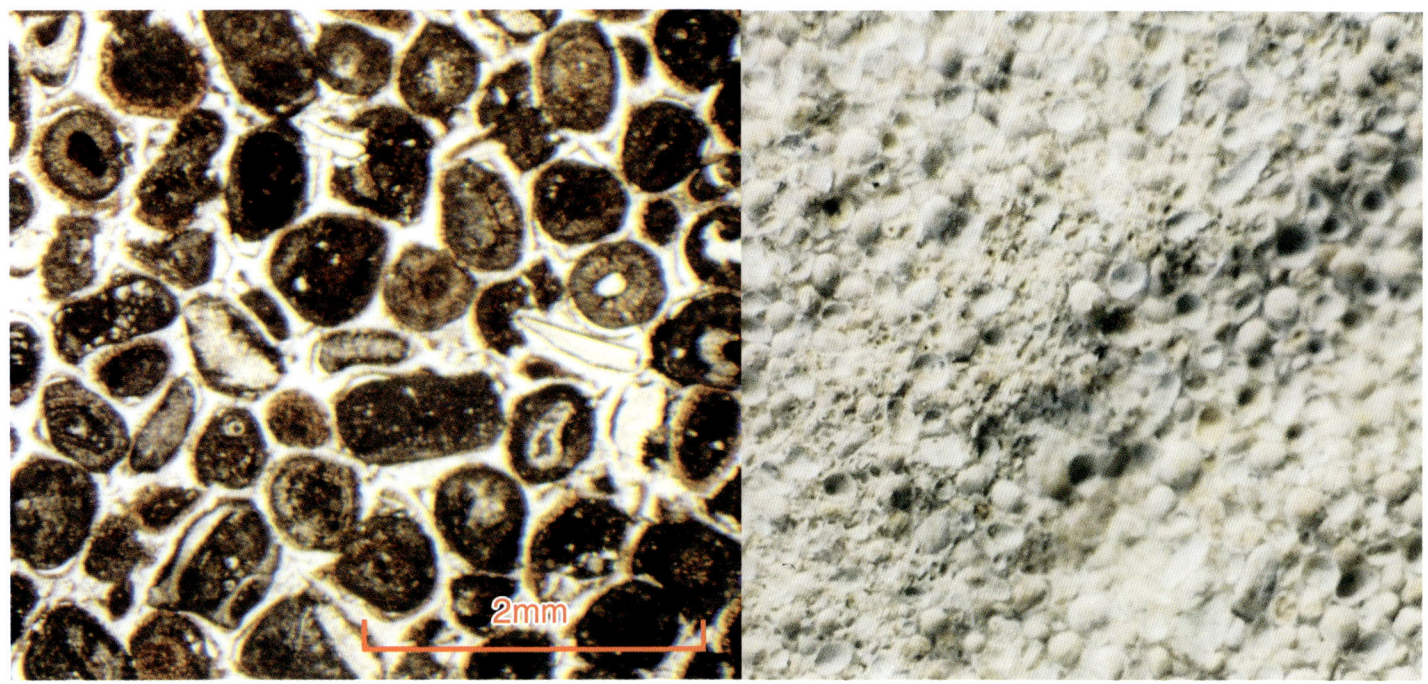

The photograph shows oolitic limestone under a microscope, with the oolites clearly visible. Photo © Earth Science Education Unit.

They are still visible under a magnifying glass. Photo © Earth Science Education Unit.

quarries will have beds of the most useful stone at different heights on the quarry face.

Chalk is a limestone and is made up of countless numbers of tiny shells called coccoliths from microscopic algae. It often contains flints, which are nodules of cryptocrystalline quartz — geologists are still uncertain how these were formed. Perhaps the best known chalk beds are seen at the White Cliffs of Dover which extend across the English Channel into northern France. In England, particularly Norfolk and Suffolk, flints, but rarely chalk, are used in building, whereas in Picardy and the Pas de Calais chalk buildings are common.

To complete the story, the best known chemically-formed limestone which is not oolitic is travertine, which was used extensively for construction in ancient Rome. When first quarried it can be soft and friable, but, like many limestones it forms a harder external layer on exposure to the atmosphere – this is known as case-hardening. It is now mostly used internally as a decorative stone, but is inconsistent, often full of holes, and not suitable for carving.

METAMORPHIC ROCKS

Marble and slate are the metamorphic stones that you are most likely to use. Marble was formed by the complete re-crystallisation of limestone at extreme temperatures and pressures, usually when the stone is buried deep in the Earth's mantle by tectonic movements close to plate boundaries, or sometimes by contact with hot rising igneous rocks. It is chemically identical to limestone. Some stones that are actually hard and polishable limestones are sometimes wrongly called marbles, but true marbles are metamorphic in origin and much denser, with low porosity and permeability.

Slate is metamorphosed shale or clay that perhaps originated as silt, and can easily be split into thin sheets. Like marble it is very fine grained and is often used for inscriptions.

The type of stone is not a guide to its age. The Earth is so old that all the processes described above will have had time to occur several times: the oldest rocks will have emerged, been worn away, deposited and compacted, returned to the earth, perhaps metamorphosed, emerged again, so many times that they are often a complete mixture of types. In addition, the tectonic forces at plate boundaries may have resulted in huge displacements: some of the world's highest mountains, for example the Canadian Rockies, were originally seabed deposits.

Many useful stones are relatively recent, in geological terms, mostly less than 500 million years old. But within that 500 million years there are building sandstones that were laid down less than 100 million years ago, and others four times older. Similarly, many European limestones date from 150–200 million years ago, when warm shallow seas were prevalent, but there are some that are more than 300 million years old. Whatever the type of stone on your bench, both its age and the forces that have acted on it are difficult to imagine.

Opposite *Marble off-cuts.*

GEOLOGY FROM A CARVER'S PERSPECTIVE

To summarise from a carver's perspective, geologists divide all rocks into three types: igneous, sedimentary and metamorphic. The only igneous stone that you may perhaps encounter is granite. It has been widely used in memorial and decorative work because it is consistent, durable and very attractive when polished. It is almost always very hard, and for this reason it is unlikely that you will be carving it with hand tools: granite masonry, carving and polishing are very mechanised processes. If you do try to cut granite, you will need chisels tipped with a particular hardness of tungsten carbide — oddly enough, the tungsten carbide needs to be softer and less brittle than that used for marble or sedimentary stones, so that it doesn't shatter.

Sandstones and limestones are both sedimentary, although sandstones are made up of silica (or sand) particles, and limestones are made from calcium carbonate. Examples of both can be used for both relief and in-the-round carving; they are often not too hard, and not expensive. So it is likely that you will be using either sandstone or limestone to start with. The key characteristic that a good carving stone for in-the-round carving must have (in addition to being not too hard and not too expensive) is that it can be cut easily in all directions. In other words, there must not be a grain or a tendency to split in one plane.

All sedimentary stones have a bedding plane — the plane that was horizontal during the deposition stage — but the useful stones have become so consistent during compaction that the bedding plane is no longer significant. Stones that have this essential characteristic are known as 'freestones'. There are sandstone freestones and limestone freestones, although the limestones are more common. When choosing a stone for carving, look for consistency and make sure that the stone you are choosing is a freestone. Finer stones, with smaller grains or oolites, are best for relief and letter cutting work because they allow detail, but coarser stones may have their own texture to add to the attraction of a larger piece.

STONE	GEOLOGICAL TYPE	CHARACTERISTICS	SOME CONTEMPORARY USES
Granite	Igneous	Hard, takes a high polish. Difficult to work with hand tools.	Internal and decorative surfaces. Monumental work.
Sandstone	Sedimentary	Varies from coarse to fine grained and from hard to soft. Often buff/khaki in colour. Does not polish. Dust mask essential.	External paving. Building stone (often locally) including carved and decorative work. Sculpture.
Limestone	Sedimentary	Also varies in grain and hardness. Often off-white or honey-coloured. Does not polish.	Building stone, including carved and decorative work. Sculpture.
Marble	Metamorphic	Very varied in colour, usually harder than sedimentary stones. Takes a high polish. Very fine grain allowing very fine detail.	Internal polished and decorative surfaces. Sculpture.
Slate	Metamorphic	Usually black or dark green. Splits easily into thin sheets. Very fine grain allowing very fine detail. Takes a high polish. Dust mask essential.	Roofing. Internal polished and decorative surfaces. Relief carving, inscriptions and monumental work.

Table showing the main stone types.

Welsh slate being prepared for an inscription.

The third geological type is metamorphic; the most common examples are marble and slate. Marble, especially pure white marble, is a freestone but in most countries it is more expensive than the sedimentary stones and usually harder. Many of the finest in-the-round carvings throughout history have been done in pure white marble because it accepts the finest detail and because it polishes quite easily. Highly coloured and patterned marbles are beautiful when polished but the colour boundaries can coincide with faults and weaknesses in the stone. Different colours may also denote different hardness or density. This may not matter when the marble is processed by machine, but can make hand carving difficult. If you want to use marble for carving it might be best to try some relief carving on a thin piece first.

Slate is also very close-grained and capable of taking fine detail but is not a freestone and it isn't usually used for in-the-round work, especially not for display outdoors. The fact that it splits easily into thin sheets has made it useful as a roofing material for centuries. Black or nearly black slate also polishes well, and is an effective medium for relief or lettering work — the cuts you make into the stone will be white or grey, contrasting with the polished stone.

A small quarry in Doulting, Somerset, UK, which supplies a predominantly local market: the usable stone is found near the surface.

CHAPTER 2

THE STONE INDUSTRY

Because of its strength and versatility, stone has been used since antiquity for load-bearing construction, and of course this structural stone has often been decorated or carved. This book describes fairly small free-standing stone carvings, but the techniques could be used equally well on stone that is to be incorporated into a building, so it might be interesting to know something about the stone industry and the people who work in it. The roles of stone mason and carver, in particular, are very close, and many of their methods and tools are the same. It may be useful to understand the traditional distinction between them, and about the way the industry is organised.

Stone that is worked from blocks and used in construction, for monumental work or for carving is known as dimension stone, and it accounts for only a small proportion of all quarried stone — most is crushed and used for aggregate and roads. Italy is by far the largest producer of dimension stone, with India and China catching up fast. Spain is also a major supplier, with the US, the UK and France all producing good stone but in relatively modest quantities. Today stone is an internationally-traded commodity, but part of the interest in stone carving comes from identifying and using local stones. In many parts of Europe, particularly where planning controls are enforced, small quarries continue to supply a local market. The photo shows a small quarry in Doulting, Somerset, UK, which supplies a predominantly local market.

Quarries producing dimension stone extract blocks of stone that are as large as possible. Traditional extraction techniques include tapping a series of wedges along a convenient fault in the quarry, or drilling a series of deep holes; ideally, the stone beds should have conveniently-spaced faults or shakes. In contrast, road-stone is often extracted by explosive as smaller pieces of stone are required.

Some dimension stone quarries have a masonry yard attached, so they can produce finished masonry; other, usually smaller, quarries may only supply rough blocks to independent yards. Quarries that produce mainly paving stone or decorative marbles and granites may have frame saws to cut the quarry blocks into large sheets of stone of various thicknesses, which are supplied to masonry yards to be made into paving or steps, or stone cladding for new buildings, or perhaps kitchen work surfaces or cemetery memorials. These sheets of stone are known as scant.

Stone yards tend to specialise in either sedimentary stones — limestone and sandstone — or in marbles, slates and granites. The sedimentary stones tend to be cheaper and more plentiful in most regions and so widely used for construction (although, as noted in the preface, in antiquity both Greece and Rome had such a plentiful supply of white marble that it was used extensively for public buildings).

Yards producing building stone need equipment to cut and handle large masonry blocks, and are noisy, mechanised places; they have stone saws, planers, polishing machines, overhead cranes and hoists, while stone masons do the things that the machines can't. Diamond-tipped water-cooled circular saws of various diameters cut the quarry blocks into sawn stone of the required size. Planers, also water-cooled, cut mouldings and sections onto sawn faces of stone, and polishing machines, their

operators wearing rubber boots or waders, slowly rub the face of the stone with finer and finer grit stones until any saw or tool marks are removed and it has a honed or fine rubbed finish. The photograph above (right) shows a large circular saw in action.

Stone masons (and sometimes carvers) work at bankers doing detailed work in difficult corners, or work on curves, or carve decorative elements. Traditionally the masons are respon-

Opposite page A corner of a masonry yard.
Above left A small water-cooled masonry saw with a diamond-tipped circular blade.
Above right A large circular saw in action.

sible for architectural features on stonework, such as mouldings, finials and pediments, whereas carvers do the decorative work such as acanthus leaves, scroll work, capitols and free carving. In practice, skilled and experienced masons and carvers cross these boundaries regularly, if only because both are in short supply. The photograph on p.24 shows a carver at work on a piece of decorated masonry.

Yards dealing mainly with marble, slate and granite are usually smaller, but more numerous. Their source material is usually scant, with its face already polished. Monumental masonry yards were often set up close to cemeteries, but these may be in decline in countries where cremation, rather than burial, is becoming more common. However, increasing numbers of yards have become specialist in supplying decorative marble,

Carver at work in a masonry yard.

granite and slate for kitchens and bathrooms. Whatever their market, they will have one or more circular saws, but with a smaller blade than the stone yards as they don't deal with quarry blocks. They will also have polishing machines, for edge and face polishing, and perhaps a letter cutting machine.

Marble masons work on decorative and curved work, and prepare stones for installation. Traditionally, carvers have found work cutting letters and inscriptions, but letter cutting and en-

graving machines now do a great deal of this work. These machines produce acceptable results for plain inscriptions in standard typefaces, but carvers are still needed for non-standard typefaces, relief carvings, work on curved surfaces, and for additions and alterations *in situ*.

Every mason and carver, whether they are specialists in marble and slate or in sedimentary stones, has a set of hand tools, but for much of the time they may use an air hammer.

This is a pneumatic cylinder held in the right hand (if you are right-handed), with a round tube in one end into which is inserted a chisel with a specially rounded shaft, held in the left hand. The hammer is powered by compressed air, and it impacts on the chisel with a very rapid hammer beat. In skilled hands the air hammer is very quick and effective (it makes mistakes quickly, too) but it makes a major contribution to the noise levels experienced in a masonry yard operating at full swing.

Masons also work on building sites, fixing the stones that have been made in the masonry yard. They are known as fixer masons, and often work under the usual time constraints and schedule pressures of a construction project. They are also highly skilled people, who often find themselves cutting stone to fit on site without the resources of the yard available to their banker mason colleagues.

Although they are noisy, wet places, masonry yards are usually welcoming to visitors; the people who work in them are always committed to the trade and have a real interest in the material they work with. Make an appointment and someone will find time to offer advice about stone, and accept a small order for some sawn stone, either a small block for in-the-round carving or a slab for relief or inscription work. Large yards dealing with building stone may have off-cuts or odd-shaped ends of blocks which they put to one side and sell cheaply to aspiring carvers — the stone used in the exercises in Chapter 4 came from such a source, as did many of the small blocks that can be seen in the background to some of the photographs in later chapters. Marble, granite and slate yards are less likely to have useful off-cuts, but small pieces 3 or 4cm (1¼ or 1½in.) thick are not expensive, and with luck might be sold at a discount to an enthusiastic and interested buyer.

CHAPTER 3

GETTING STARTED

EQUIPMENT

T his chapter describes how to get organised with a place to work, some tools, and a piece of stone. First, the three essential health and safety rules:

- always wear eye protection when cutting stone
- always wear a dust mask when cutting sandstone or slate
- always observe the usual precautions that apply to moving and lifting heavy objects, and get help if in any doubt.

A PLACE TO WORK

A dedicated stone workshop is ideal, especially for in-the-round (3D) work where larger volumes of stone are being cut away. Otherwise work outside, with a cover or awning for when it rains — all the work illustrated in this book was done in a small patio area at the back of my house in London. A place shaded from direct sunlight and facing north (in the northern hemisphere) is ideal; the light should be consistent and free of shadows for as long as possible each day.

Opposite *The author at work on a piece of Portland limestone.*

Working with stone always produces dust and small chippings. Volumes of dust are quite small when carving letters and inscriptions, and much greater when working in the round. Whatever you are carving, eye protection is *essential* whenever you pick up a chisel.

All the pieces described in this book were made on a mason's bench, or *banker*. It is cheap and easy to make. All you need are eight builder's blocks, or breeze blocks, a paving slab and a piece of carpet. The blocks and the slab are made of concrete and available at all building suppliers; carpet shops will often sell carpet samples which can be cut to size.

The banker in the photo on the next page is made from blocks that are 44 x 22 x 14cm (17 x 9 x 5½in.). The paving slab is 45 x 45 x 3.8cm (18 x 18 x 1½in.). This arrangement gives a working height of 90cm (35½in.) which is right for most people, whether standing or sitting on a high stool. The banker needs to be positioned so that you can easily walk round it, and work at all four sides — sometimes, when the stone on the banker is heavy, it's easier to move you than it. The banker should be built on a firm and level surface, either paving or concrete; there is no need to use cement or an adhesive to join the blocks, or the slab to the blocks, as the structure is very firm, stable and strong.

The banker.

SOME TOOLS TO START WITH

There are some limestones that are soft enough to be carved with wood chisels, but usually masons and stone carvers use specialist tools. The most obvious difference is that chisels for wood work have a wooden handle and are used with a wooden mallet, whereas an entire stone chisel, shaft and blade, is made of steel. Carvers usually use them with a steel hammer or dummy (although masons often use a wooden or nylon mallet). A second difference is that stone chisels are beveled and sharpened on both sides of the blade, whereas wood tools are sharpened on one side only. A third difference, as noted below, is that many masons and stone carvers now use tungsten-tipped chisels, which are not used for working in wood.

The first two worked examples in this book use pieces of slab stone and produce two-dimensional, or relief, carvings. The carving needs to be accurate, and the chisels need to be quite small and sharp. The third and fourth worked examples described in Chapter 5 use a larger block of stone to produce a three dimensional or in-the-round sculpture, and for these you will need bigger and heavier tools to shift larger volumes of stone. The two sets are often known as carver's tools and mason's tools. Here we will look at the carver's tools that you will need and leave the larger tools to Chapter 5.

All stone chisels, mason's or carver's, can be bought with traditional firesharp tips which are drawn out and tempered by hand, or with tungsten carbide tips. The advantages of the firesharp chisels are that they can be drawn out to a finer tip, they don't shatter when dropped on the sharp end, and they are easy to sharpen. Their main disadvantage is that they lose their edge quickly, especially when using harder stones and particularly sandstones. Tungsten carbide tools, on the other hand, stay sharp for a very long time, but once broken or shattered they can't be drawn out again. They also need special equipment to sharpen them, either 'green' sharpening blocks for hand sharpening or (much the quickest way) a special 'green' wheel for electric bench grinders.

(Above) *Some light carving chisels and a dummy.*
(Right) *5mm, 10mm and 13mm carver's chisels.*

The choice is yours, and over time you will probably accumulate some of each, but to start with it might be best to buy a few tungsten carbide tools, especially if you already have an electric grinder that will accept (or already has) a 'green' sharpening wheel. For the preliminary exercise, the Celtic knot pattern carving and the lettering exercise (Project 2), you will need:

TOOL LIST

- Eye protection and a dust mask
- A steel head hammer weighing between 0.7–0.9kg (1½lb and 2lb)
- 0.7kg (1lb) dummy (optional)
- 5mm (³⁄₁₆ in.) chisel

- 10mm (⅜in.) chisel
- 13mm (½in.) chisel
- A point
- Silicon carbide abrasive block 80 grade
- A claw tool (optional)

If you can, try the hammers for weight and feel before deciding which one to buy. Carvers use a traditional hammer with two flat faces; some prefer a short handle — if the handle is made of wood you can cut it to the length you want. Specialist letter cutters often use dummys, which have cylindrical heads and short handles, and usually weigh about 0.45kg (1lb). If you intend to make a number of inscriptions, it would be worth buying a dummy, otherwise, a carver's hammer will be fine.

A point is simply a piece of metal sharpened to a point on the end of a shaft; the pointed end consists of four tapering faces. It is used for clearing stone out of the way quickly, but must be used carefully as it is difficult to control. You need a carver's point with a shaft diameter of 1cm (⅜in.), rather than a mason's punch, which is a bigger and heavier version of the same tool. A claw tool looks a bit like a row of small points and it does a similar job. One isn't really needed for these relief exercises although a larger mason's claw, available in different widths and with either fixed or replaceable tips, will be useful for the larger carvings in Chapter 5. Scribers are about the size and shape of an ordinary pencil and not designed to be hit with a hammer; they are used to mark a straight line in the same way as a pencil except that the stone is physically engraved slightly.

Silicon carbide abrasive blocks (the trade name is Carborundum) are made of the same material as the wheels for electric grinders, but in rectangular shape for hand use, 20 x 5 x 2.5cm (8 x 2 x 1in.) when new. They are used for smoothing the carved stone to a finished surface: an 80 grade block is probably the most useful for limestone and sandstone, but 60 grade and 120 grade blocks are handy as well. There is a photograph of a new block being used in the preliminary exercise in Chapter 4. Carvers often need small pieces of abrasive blocks, in odd shapes, to fit into the difficult corners of the work. Unfortunately, you can't buy these small pieces, so you have to break bits off the block and rub them into the shape you need, or collect the bits that break off when you drop a block. Soon you will have a collection of small pieces of Carborundum, partly worn into useful shapes.

CHOOSING STONE

In all cases, look carefully at the stone you are buying. Pick it up, smell it (some limestones smell fishy!), scratch it with a chisel if you can. If you are buying a block for in-the-round carving, bounce the bottom of a large chisel (the part you hit with the hammer) on it. The stone should ring. If it doesn't there may be a hidden vent that might cause the stone to break or split, usually when you have almost finished the work — this happened to the original version of the carving worked in Project 4.

If you are buying stone for an inscription or for a relief carving (such as the knot pattern carving and the letter cutting examples in this book), it will probably need to be a specific size and cut from a sheet or scant. If your carving is in sandstone or limestone, you will need the working surface to be fine rubbed, to make it perfectly flat and to remove all traces of saw marks. It should be 4 or 5cm (1½ or 2in.) thick. If you are using slate or marble you will probably want it to be polished on the seen surface for maximum effect, and the stone should be at least 3cm (1¼in.) thick.

Unless you have a local stone that you want to use, or have an interest in a particular stone, start with a limestone. If you live in Western Europe, choose one of the oolitic freestones that are found in a band from southern England to Normandy: one of the Bath stones such as Stokes Ground, or Portland stone (which was used extensively to rebuild London after the Great Fire of 1666), or one of the very fine French stones such as Richmont or Anstrude. In the US Indiana limestone is widely available and good for carving, with stone also available in Wisconsin, Alabama, Iowa and Kansas. Alabaster, serpentine and soapstone are also available to carvers in the US and in Scandinavia, as well as the Near and Middle East.

The preliminary exercise described in the next chapter will not give you a finished object, so use an inexpensive piece of stone. The cheapest piece of stone is probably a paving stone — 30cm (12in.) square is ideal. Choose one that is stone, not marble, and at least 4cm (1½in.) thick. It can be sandstone or limestone,

Stone off-cuts from the author's yard. The only stone paid for is the Portland stone panel resting on the floor. On the bench are (from the left) two blocks of Bath stone, one of Richmont Crème and three of Richmont Blu, and one of Portland stone.

imported or local, and will probably be intended for use outside on patios or driveways, rather than inside.

The stone should have a flat and smooth top surface, known as a honed or fine rubbed finish. This means that saw marks on the face of the stone have been mechanically rubbed away — any saw marks that remain on the sides can easily be removed with a sili-con carbide abrasive block. And finally, it must be genuine natural stone: a lot of cheaper paving is made from cast, or artificial, stone, which can look very like the real thing but is made of concrete.

So now you have a banker, some tools and a piece of stone. The next chapter looks briefly at the physical process of carving stone, and then describes a straightforward exercise.

Ready to begin the first exercise.

CHAPTER 4

GETTING STARTED

TECHNIQUES

Carving stone is a process of controlled breaking away of stone or bursting; uncontrolled bursting is known as plucking or flushing. A great deal of stone carving technique is concerned with controlling the bursting process and it is important to understand that, when hit by a chisel blade, stone will always burst away in the direction of least resistance. So always make sure that there is a greater mass of stone beneath or behind the chisel blade than there is on top or in front of it, so that the stone on top or in front of the blade bursts away; this principle applies whether you are hitting great lumps of stone away or taking off tiny pieces of stone, as in this preliminary exercise.

When making the first cut into a stone block (except when using a pitcher, see Chapter 5), you can't hold the chisel blade at right angles to the surface of the stone because the stone is just as likely to burst on one side of the blade as on the other. So in the exercise described below, and in all the projects later in the book, the first cut into the block is made with a small chisel with the blade held at an angle of about 45 degrees to the surface of the stone. This ensures that the stone will burst upwards from the chisel. When the 45 degree cut is extended to form a line, it is known as chasing a line, and chasing is a key stone carving skill. This line is used to define the edge or outline of the carving, and is also the essential skill used for carving inscriptions (Project 2).

Having chased the lines that delineate the carving, subsequent cuts must still ensure that the stone bursts away in the direction that you intend. So never try to cut too much at one go, so you avoid the stone plucking beneath the chisel blade — it's better to make several passes as necessary. Always be particularly careful at the end or corner of a piece of stone — remember to stop some distance from the end and cut back into the mass of stone from the opposite direction.

The stone used in the photographs in this chapter is a sandstone paving slab (as you will probably notice, it was used for an abandoned project and turned upside down for this exercise). This slab is from the Crosland Hill quarry in Yorkshire, UK, but good quality (and perhaps cheaper) sandstone slabs from China and India are now widely obtainable from good building suppliers or landscaping outlets; limestone slabs may also be available. If you decide to use sandstone for this exercise (or for any of the others) always wear a dust mask as well as eye protection. This is because the tiny, sharp particles of quartz can cause lung damage when inhaled.

Chasing the lines.   *Cutting back in.*

This preliminary exercise is designed to show you some of the skills involved in accurate stone carving. It involves cutting a notch, or rebate, along one side of the stone. The first stage is to cut an angled top edge; this is known as a chamfer. The second stage then deepens the chamfer to form the rebate.

If you are right handed, you will naturally hold the chisel with your left hand. When I was at masonry college in the '70s, the carving teacher told us that we should hold the chisel as gently as if we were holding a bird. In other words, firmly enough to prevent it being knocked out of your hand with each hammer blow, but not so firmly that your knuckles turn white. Use the hammer gently and fairly rapidly, but don't try to take off too much stone with each stroke.

Wearing eye protection and a dust mask if you are using sandstone, make two pencil or scriber lines 10mm (⅜in.) from the edge of the stone, one on the top surface and one on the side. If you do use a scriber, run a sharp pencil along the scriber mark, to make it easier to see.

Using a 4 or 5mm chisel (³⁄₁₆in.) with the blade held at 45 degrees, chase both lines. Use light beats of the hammer and don't dig in too far: the chase should be perhaps 2 or 3mm (about ⅛in.) deep, less than the width of the blade.

When you get to 50mm (2in.) or so from the end, stop and cut back in from the opposite direction, to avoid knocking the corner of the stone off. Be careful to follow the line as accurately as you can and don't allow the chase to wander across it.

Having chased the top and bottom lines that mark the extent of the rebate, you now need to form the chamfer by

Cutting the chamfer — chisel angle.

The finished chamfer.

cutting away the stone between them. The easiest way to do this is to use a larger chisel, with a 13mm (5in.) tip, held at a 45 degree angle. Again, don't try to do it in one pass: you will probably pluck the stone beyond the chased lines or too deep below the chisel. Just take off 2mm (about ¹⁄₁₆in.) each time — it will take three or four passes to finish the chamfer.

When the chamfer is finished you can check to see how accurate you have been by resting a ruler or straight edge along it and looking between the straight edge and the stone to see if there are any low or high spots. If you have been reasonably accurate, a few passes with a silicon carbide abrasive block along

the chamfer will finish the job. If not, try the exercise again on another edge.

The next stage is to make the rebate. You need to chase into the stone along your original line, which now forms the junction between the chamfer and the top flat surface of the stone, and again along the original line between the chamfer and the side of the stone. As before, the blade should be at 45 degrees to the surface of the stone — but the chamfer is already at 45 degrees, so this time the angle of the blade is vertical for the upper chase, and horizontal for the lower one.

Cutting the upper chase into the chamfer.

Cutting the lower chase into the chamfer.

Once again, use a small chisel, and don't go deeper than the blade width. You are now left with some rough stone between the chased lines, and this is a good opportunity to try using a point. Remember that plucking is hard to control when using a point because it has no blade to control the direction of the action. On the other hand it is quick to use, and the stone will not burst beyond the two chased lines if you are not too heavy with the hammer. So use the point to remove some of the stone

(not forgetting to stop before the end and reverse direction) and then use your 10mm (⅜in.) chisel to slowly work off the two sides of the rebate. As before, remember not to take too much stone off with each pass.

Finally, use a silicon carbide abrasive block to rub away any slight imperfections and tool marks in the rebate. The finished exercise should look something like the stone in the photograph opposite.

Starting to work the rebate.   *The tooled rebate.*

Using the silicon carbide abrasive block.   *The finished exercise.*

PROJECT 1
A CELTIC KNOT PATTERN

The first of the four worked projects in this book is a Celtic knotwork panel. Celtic art is a fascinating subject in its own right, and there are several books devoted to the characteristic interlaced, or knotwork, patterns: George Bain's book *Celtic Art — the Methods of Construction* was first published in 1951 and has been reprinted regularly ever since, and more recently Courtney Davis has written and illustrated a series of practical guides to Celtic designs.

Fairly straightforward knotwork panels (relief carvings, essentially two-dimensional) are a good place for a carver to gain some experience in using stone carving tools, and to get a feeling of what it feels like to cut into a piece of stone. They don't need to be complex, and their regularity enables you to concentrate on the stone, rather than on the design — the width of the band or ribbon and its height above the background, remains the same. You just have to be careful to get the 'overs' and the 'unders' right, but that happens at the end of the process.

The particular design carved in this chapter is taken from George Bain's book; his source was the Book of Kells (Plate XIX) where it is drawn 6mm (¼in.) long! As well as being used for book illustration, Celtic knot patterns carved in stone were sometimes used on cemetery memorials, especially in Victorian and Edwardian England; the endless ribbon signifies eternity.

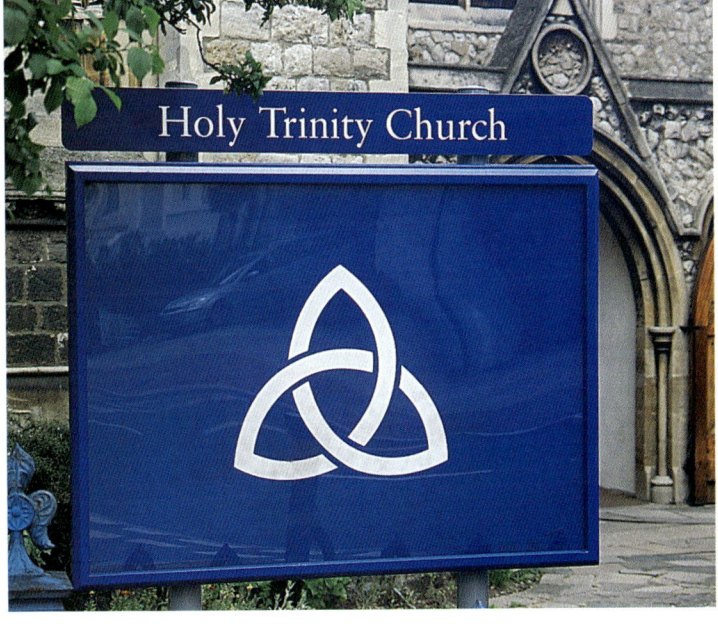

Opposite A headstone in a south London graveyard.
Right A simple Celtic knot pattern.

The blank stone.   *The outline design.*

The stone shown in the photographs is a small panel of Portland stone quarried in Dorset, UK. Portland stone is a fine white limestone, although this piece is quite shelly. It measures 43 x 22 x 5cm (about 17 x 8¾ x 2in.) and was cut from an external stair tread that was damaged. You could use a square paving stone like the one used in Chapter 4 (if you use sandstone remember always to wear a dust mask) but you would obviously need a different design to the one illustrated here — many are shown in the books mentioned above or you may have your own ideas for designs. We will be carving an inscription in marble or slate in Project 2, so use sandstone or limestone for this project.

As with the preliminary exercise in Chapter 4, this carving starts with drawing. Accurate drawing is essential. Draw with a hard pencil directly onto the stone, and don't pick up a hammer and chisel until you are quite sure that the drawing is absolutely correct — time spent drawing the outline of the work is never wasted, because if your outline is accurate you just have to follow the line when carving, and you will be able to concentrate on your stone cutting technique and not have to make adjustments to the design as you go.

First draw the basic design onto the stone. Then decide how wide the ribbon will be (15mm, or ⅝in in this example, although you might choose a different width) and draw the complete design — the lines of the outline design now lie in the centre of the ribbon. The curves are drawn freehand; mistakes drawn on stone can be rubbed out using a fine silicon carbide abrasive stone.

These are the lines that the carving will follow, and it is

(Above) *The complete design.*
(Above right) *The first cut! Note the angle of the chisel blade.*
(Right) *Chasing the outline.*

important to make sure that the width of the band is the same everywhere. Don't try to identify the 'overs' and 'unders' yet. Double check that everything looks right, and once it is, it's time to begin to carve the stone.

The first stage is to begin to cut back the background, leaving the ribbon raised. The background needs to be 8 or 9mm (⅜in.) deeper than the ribbon. Wearing eye protection, chase the outline in just the same way as you did in the earlier exercise, except this time many of the lines to chase are curved. Don't try to make the initial cut more than 2 or 3mm (⅛in.) deep — use a small 4 or 5mm (³⁄₁₆in.) chisel and a carving hammer or dummy used very lightly.

Remember that stone carving is essentially a process of bursting stone away from the block in a controlled way; by

making the chase with an angled blade you will ensure that the stone bursts away from the ribbon. Later we will come back and cut the sides of the ribbon vertically, after some of the background stone has been cleared away.

The second chase.   *Using the point.*

Don't chase across the ribbon! At this stage just chase round all the ribbon outline; in other words you are chasing the outline of small squares or triangles at the outsides of the piece. When all the outline has been chased, start to clear away the background, or lower, areas using a point. Start on the areas within the carving; leave the edges of the stone until later. Continue using a dummy or light carving hammer, although you may be confident enough to strike the point a bit harder than you did when chasing.

You will not be able to achieve the full depth in one operation. To begin with, cut all the background areas down to the depth of the first chase. Then chase the outline again to the full depth, using a larger chisel — 10mm (⅜in.) — but again using an angled blade, and cut away the background for the second time with a point. Then use the same chisel held with the blade flat to work off the stone that the point left raised and to arrive at about the right depth. There is no need to try for a perfectly smooth finish because we will leave the surface finish of the background until the end.

Working the outline of the band to vertical sides.

Stabbing downwards.

Although most of the stone in the centre of the squares and triangles has been cleared away, the ribbon itself gets wider as it gets deeper because of the angle of the blade when chasing. So go back to the outline of the band and cut the sides vertically. Because all the background stone has been removed, you can be confident that the stone will burst in the right direction — away from the raised band. You still need to be careful and use small, light beats of the dummy; even so, you may not be able to achieve vertical edges in one pass; it depends on the hardness and consistency of your stone. When this has been done, you will need to finish working the background areas roughly flat, and roughly to the same depth of about 8 or 9mm (⅜in.).

Making the sides of the ribbon vertical is difficult. One technique that is sometimes useful, especially in corners, is to stab directly downwards with a sharp chisel.

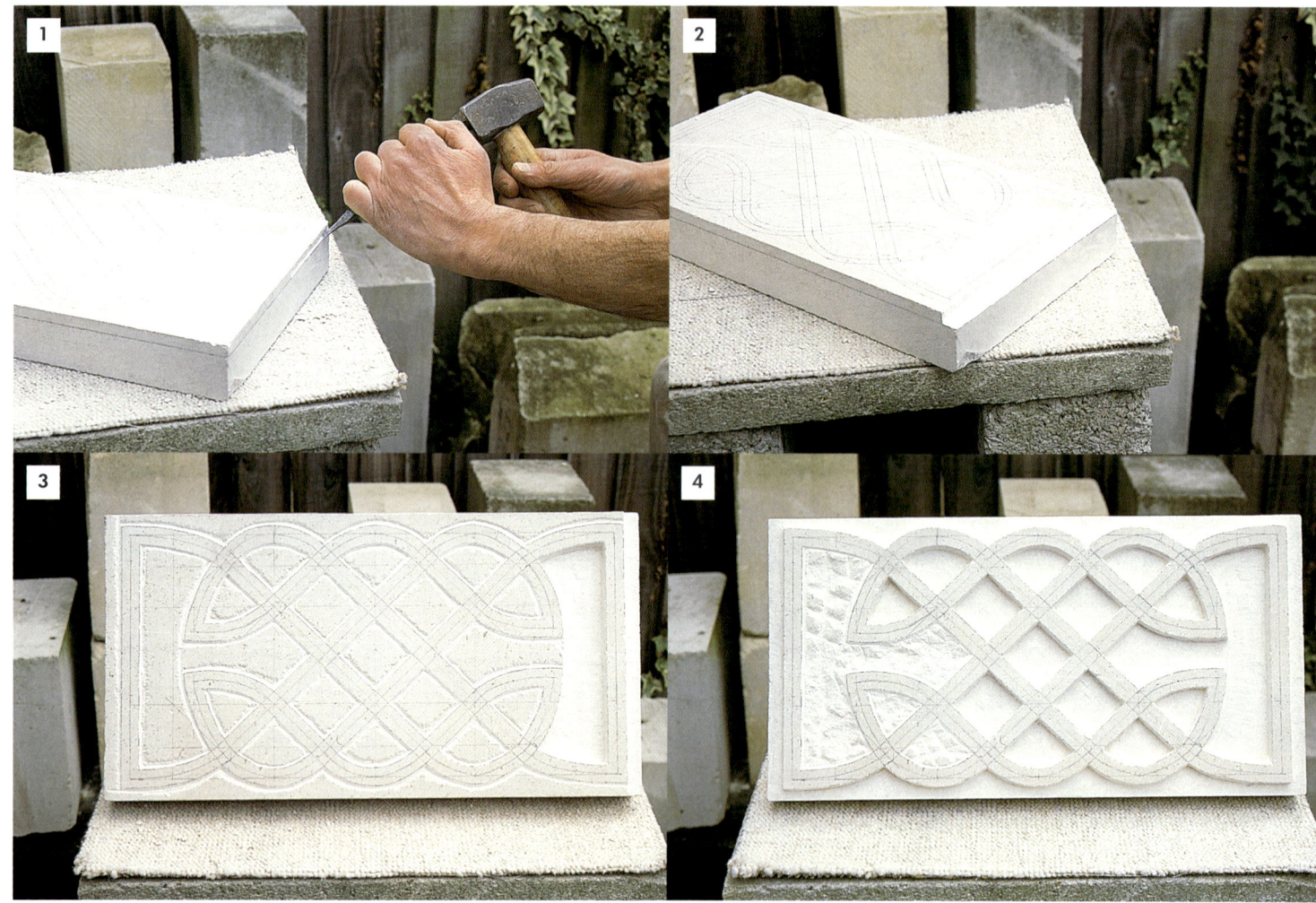

To finish carving the outline you need to cut away the outside edges of the stone up to the outside of the ribbon, to the same depth as the background areas within the carving. For the short sides with straight edges, this is done in exactly the same way as the preliminary exercise in Chapter 4. The longer sides with the curved ribbon line will take a bit longer but by now you will be getting used to using the same sequence of carving: first chasing and clearing, then chasing again to the full depth and clearing again, then working the bottom surface roughly flat, and finally working the edges vertical. Then you need to finish carving away the background.

Now it is finally time to work in the 'overs' and 'unders'. Remember that if the line went 'under' at a particular intersection, it must go 'over' at all the adjacent ones — the intersections always alternate. Using a pencil, carefully mark the ribbon at the crossovers.

Then take a sharp chisel, 13mm (½in.) is ideal in this example, and very gently stab downwards along the outside of the pencil lines of the 'over' ribbon, at a slight angle from the vertical to make the stone burst in the required direction. Using the same chisel, but held flat, cut the 'under' ribbon towards the stab cut: as long as you are fairly gentle the stab will prevent the stone plucking beyond it. Make several passes, each cutting away less than

1 *Chasing an edge line.*
2 *The finished edge.*
3 *The stone fully chased and partly worked.*
4 *The stone with background mostly removed.*
5 *The 'overs' and 'unders' marked with pencil.*
6 *Stabbing down at the crossovers.*
7 *Cutting the under ribbon.*

1mm (⅟₃₂in.). Repeat this several times, until the 'under' bands have been cut down to half the depth of the background. Then you will need to make the sides of the 'over' ribbon vertical where you stabbed down by carefully chasing across. Remember to turn and cut in from the other direction to prevent bursting — this applies even though the chase is only 15mm (⅝in.) long.

To make a contrasting texture in the background between the bands, try 'sparrowpecking'. You will need a point. The point is sharpened from a four-sided shaft, rather than a round one, and all you do is hold the point downwards and tap it with a light hammer or a dummy. This is the one time when you do want the stone to burst in random directions! The point should not be too

sharp, to prevent the stone surface ending up looking as if it is covered with pin pricks. Try to develop a quick light beat with the hammer, at the same time moving the point between each beat.

Sparrowpecking gives an interesting texture and means you don't need to work the background to a fine finish — it is often used as the background to an inscription using raised letters. Be careful not to hit the point too often in the same place. It is easy to peck away too much stone in the middle of an area, so it may be necessary to work a bit more near the edges after the first application. Sparrowpecking the outside of the carving is difficult because of the danger of bursting the stone on the edge, so leave a margin of smooth stone next to the edge; but

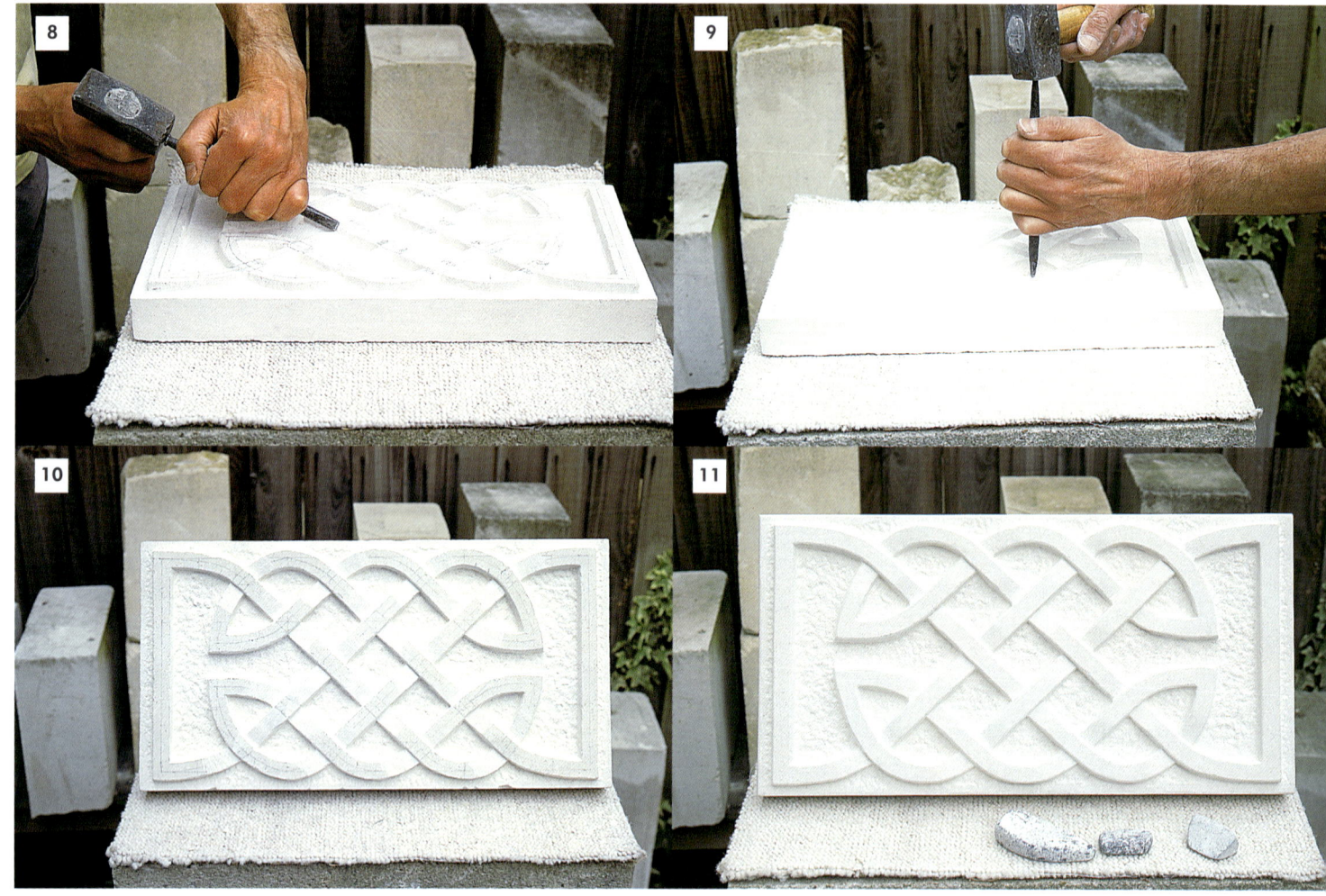

8 *Finishing the over ribbon.*
10 *Sparrowpecking finished.*

9 *Sparrowpecking.*
11 *The finished stone with some silicon carbide abrasive pieces.*

even so you may burst the edge, as you may be able to see in the photograph. We will look at stone repair techniques in Chapter 6.

At this point you need to look critically at the carving as a whole. Check that the sides of the ribbons are reasonably vertical; you may have to do some work at the intersections, to make sure that the ribbon is the same width at each side.

Relief carvings in limestone and sandstone do not usually have sharp edges (or arrises, as masons call them) — the

stone is not hard and fine enough, and the edges often have small flushes in them, caused by a small piece of shell or other imperfection being exposed. Use a silicon carbide abrasive block to gently round off the outer edges of the carving. Then use it to rub off any remaining pencil lines on the ribbon and smooth out any remaining tool marks on the top and sides of the ribbon. Finally, use a small piece of silicon carbide abrasive to gently round off the edges of the ribbon.

SOME EXAMPLES OF CELTIC KNOT PATTERN CARVING

Above *A complex single-band pattern. Carved in limestone, 1880.*

Right *A memorial covered in different knot patterns. Carved in granite, 1896.*

Inset *A simple repeated design. Carved in limestone, 1916.*

Robin Golden-Hann cutting letters for a large inscription on the memorial ledger slate for Sir Edward Heath.

PROJECT 2
CARVING AN INSCRIPTION

In the days before letter carving machines, inscriptions were all made by stone carvers, it was a regular source of work. Now a lot of routine work is done by machine but the best and most important work is still done by hand. All work in a non-standard typeface, on a curved surface or on any stone that can't be brought to a workshop has to be carved by hand. Carvers often call the work 'letter cutting', which is an accurate description but doesn't give much idea of the skill and patience required to do it.

Inscriptions are often carved onto marble and slate because of the durability of the carving and the very fine level of detail that can achieved. The United States maintains 124,000 grave-markers for its soldiers killed and buried overseas in the two world wars of the 20th century, all in fine Italian marble, but fine sandstones and limestones are also used for this purpose. Around the world there are more than a million headstones commemorating British and Commonwealth servicemen and women who died in the world wars, almost all of them made from limestone.

The example in this chapter is carved onto a small piece of Italian black slate, polished, measuring 23 x 16.5 x 3cm (9 x 6½ x 1¼in.). The work is done flat on the mason's banker, and the carpet provides enough friction to prevent the stone moving too much; however, some carvers prefer to use an easel made from a larger piece of flat stone held at a convenient angle.

When carving onto slate or marble it is often a good idea to paint the surface of the stone with a water-based emulsion paint, matt white. Pencil or carbon paper marks are hard to see on slate, which is usually black or grey or sometimes dark green, and white marble is often too highly polished to accept a pencil mark. Once finished, you can wash the paint off again.

If you have been commissioned to do an inscription you may be provided with a full-sized drawing; more often you will be expected to design and lay out the work, accepting responsibility for the centring of the inscription, the spacing between the letters and words, and the size of the letters. This design has to be done full size on good quality drawing paper. When you are happy with it, cut the paper to the size of the stone and using adhesive tape, attach carbon or copy paper to the back of the drawing, carbon face outwards. If possible, leave the edges of the drawing free of carbon paper. Then fix the drawing to the emulsion-painted stone, again using adhesive tape, and draw the outline of the inscription again, so that it transfers to the stone.

The carving itself is done very carefully and slowly, using the lightest of blows from a dummy or hammer. Slate is difficult to carve because, being layered, it flushes and plucks very easily; marble, especially when grainy or crystalline, is also demanding to control. But with patience and care and a bit of practice, beautiful clear lettering can be achieved.

1 *The blank stone.*
2 *The transferred outline.*
3 *Cutting into the letter.*

4 *Stabbing at an intersection.*
5 *Smoothing the cut by hand.*
6 *The finished carving, with the white paint to be washed off.*

The carving is done in a V-shape by chasing one side of the letter then reversing the angle of the chisel and chasing the other side. Many inscriptions are done in letters derived from Trajan or Times Roman fonts, and these have different thickness of line for different parts of each letter. If parts of a letter are wider, they are also deeper because the angle of the V-shape has to be constant.

As with any stone carving, stone will pluck or burst in an uncontrolled way when you try to take off too much stone at once. Particularly with the wider parts of the letters, don't try to get to the pencil line in one pass, but clear away some of the stone in the middle of the letter first, so when you do cut to the line there is less stone in front of the chisel — remember that the greater the mass of stone in front of (or on top of) the chisel blade, the greater the chance of plucking behind the blade. When carving the thinner parts of the letters, or generally with smaller letters, there may not be enough space to do

this, but then the V-cut is not so deep, so there is less chance of plucking anyway.

Again, as with any stone carving, always cut into the mass of stone. Serifs should be worked from the tail in towards the letter, and when approaching a crossing point where the first line has already been cut, turn round and cut back into the stone. Intersections need particular care; it's sometimes a good idea to mark both sides of the crossing lines with a gentle stab downwards with a sharp chisel, or by a short scribed line — this can help to prevent flushing.

The letters in the example above are about 5cm (2in.) high. Most of the work was done with a home-made 0.7 kg (1lb) dummy and a 5mm (³⁄₁₆in.) fish-tailed chisel, and some finishing work in the wider parts of the letters was done with an 8mm (⁵⁄₁₆in.) chisel. Fish-tailed chisels (where the shaft immediately behind the blade has been partly cut away) are useful for detailed carving because the shaft does not contact the

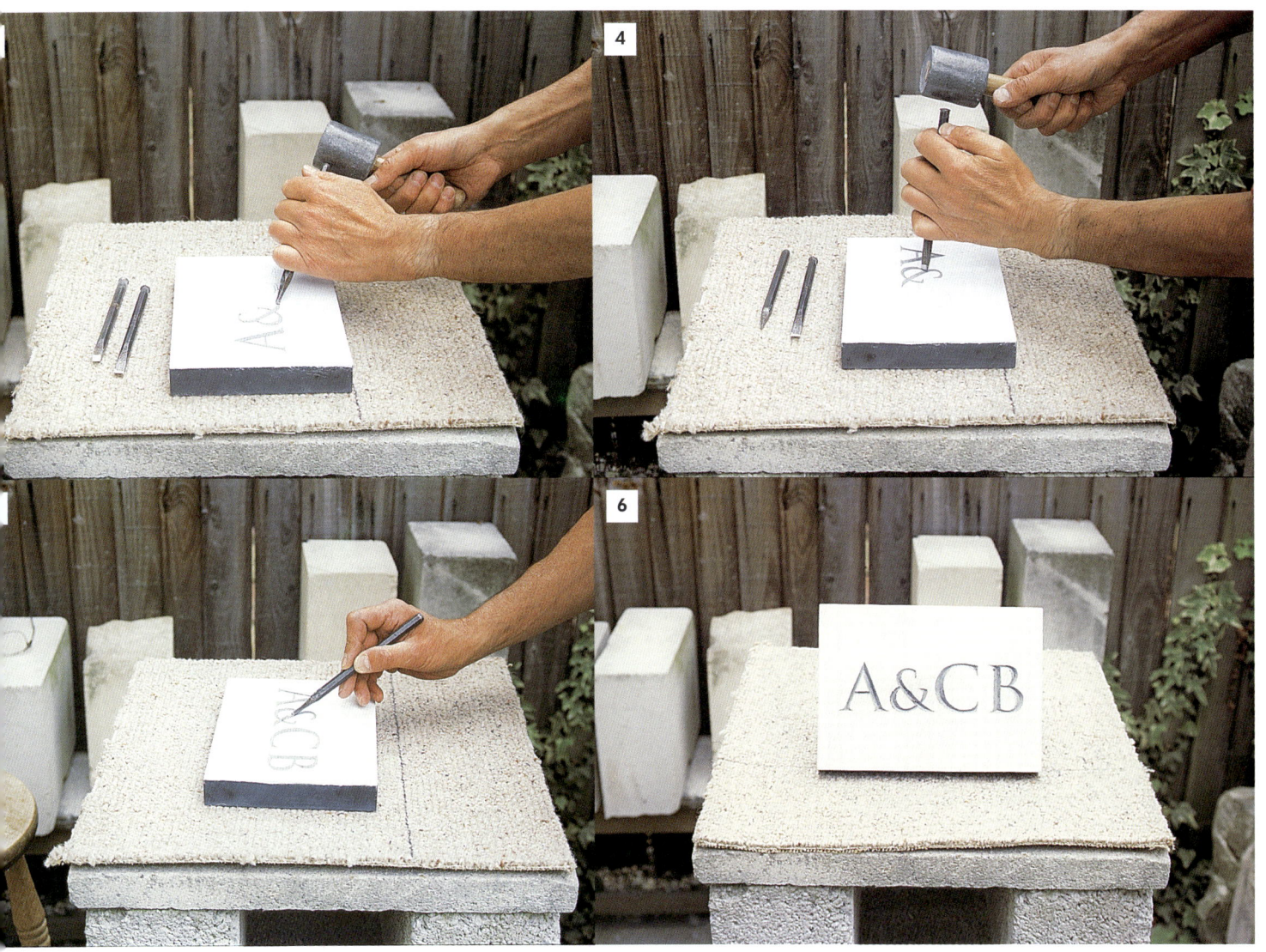

adjacent stone or (in the case of carving inscriptions) the edge of the letter. As always, wear eye protection, and for slate or sandstone a dust mask.

One advantage of using slate for inscriptions is that the inscribed letters are a lighter grey colour than the polished surface of the slate (or lighter green if you are using green slate), so it's easy to read the inscription. Inscriptions in white marble or light-coloured limestone are often not easy to read and so the letters are sometimes gilded (covered with gold leaf) or painted. Enamel paint is used, often black (or white if an in-

scription in slate needs to be painted), although many other colours are available from model shops and suppliers. In a commercial marble workshop the paint would be quickly applied, allowed to dry and the surface of the stone then re-polished or re-honed by machine. If these facilities are not available, you will need to apply the paint very carefully, with a small fine brush, taking great care not to go over the edges of the letters. One coat is usually enough.

This tree commemorates the life of

HENRY WOLF

1925 – 2005

Art Director
Photographer &
Artist

FRIEND TO THE
CHRISTIE-MILLER
FAMILY
OVER 40 YEARS

QUE TE QUIE
IENTO VERD
OBRE LA MAI
N LA MONTA

Arthur & Margaret
BATEMAN
1923·2006·1929·198
TO LOVE & BE LOVE

SOME EXAMPLES OF CARVED INSCRIPTIONS

This page, above *Memorial carved by Robin Golden-Hann.*
Top right & bottom right *Inscriptions by Fergus Wessel.*
Opposite page, top & centre *Two alphabets carved in stone.*
Top right *Stones in workshop by Fergus Wessel.*
Bottom left *Example of lettering by Fergus Wessel.*
Bottom right *Carved headstone by Robin Golden-Hann.*

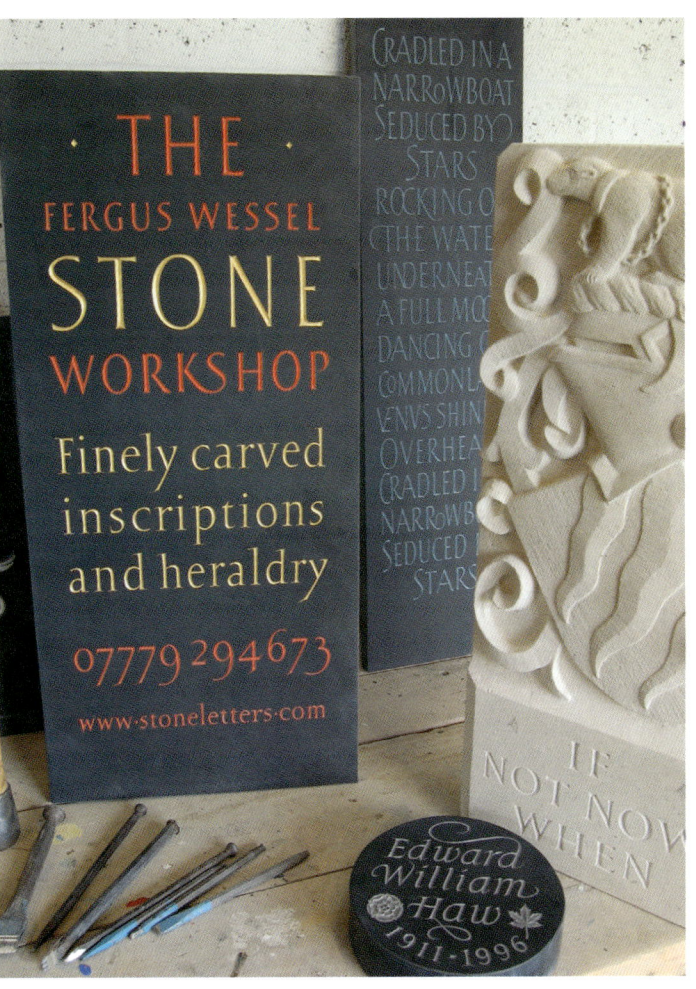

Some tools for carving in the round, and a small block of French limestone.

CHAPTER 5

TOOLS AND TECHNIQUES FOR 3D WORK

TOOLS FOR LARGER WORK

Unlike woodcarvers, who seem to have dozens of chisels, all slightly different and all absolutely essential, stone carvers use relatively few hand tools. Of course they may collect or inherit many more but the chances are that they use a small number of tools most of the time, and have others that they rarely pick up.

Three traditional mason's tools that are very useful for removing large volumes of stone quickly are the pitcher, the punch and the claw. The pitcher is unusual because its leading edge is not sharp, although it is slightly splayed. When correctly used it sends a shock through the stone in the same direction as the handle is held, causing quite large pieces to fall away, so it is useful when starting to carve a piece from a sawn block. It only works against a flat (sawn) stone face. The leading edge is held flat against the side of the block, with the handle perpendicular to the block, and the tool is struck hard, once or perhaps twice, with a 1kg (2lb approx.) hammer. The pitcher can do a lot of work for you — used correctly, it removes more stone from a block more quickly than any other tool.

The punch and the claw are used conventionally, pushed through the stone with repeated hammer blows. The punch is a larger version of the carver's point, and is used to get close to the depth or line of the carving. The claw is often used after the punch to clear away the stone left by the punch and to arrive at a close approximation of the required line in the carving — some sculptors use a claw to give the finished texture to a piece. The picture opposite (top) shows the pitcher, punch and claw tool with replaceable bit. Unless you expect to use them quite a lot on hard stone, there is no need to buy tungsten tipped versions of the pitcher and punch; mason's claws are bought with replaceable steel bits, as in the photograph — the one shown is 2.5cm (1in.) wide, and they are also available at 4.5cm (1¾ in.) wide.

Mason's chisels are essentially the same as carver's chisels, but with larger blades and thicker shafts. They are available with either tungsten carbide or firesharp tips, and the advantages and disadvantages of each were described in Chapter 3. In addition, mason's chisels are available with two different shaft shapes, known as hammer headed and mallet headed. Mallet headed chisels and hammer headed chisels are shown in the picture opposite.

Mallets are available in hardwood or nylon in various weights. Some masons like to use them for the finishing stages of a job — they like the slight bounce and they use a slower

(Above left) *Heavier tools and a hammer.*
(Above right) *Claw tools.*
(Inset) *Silicone carbide pieces.*

rhythm of one or two beats each second, moving the blade of the chisel back from the stone between beats, to check on progress and prevent the chisel digging in. Hammers are also available in different weights and are easily obtained from ordinary hardware outlets — the photo shows a beechwood mallet 0.75kg (about 1.6lb) and a mason's hammer 0.9kg (2lb).

It is expensive to buy sets of mallet-headed chisels and hammer-headed chisels, so to start with stick to the hammer-headed tools. There is no reason why you can't use a mallet with a hammer-headed chisel, especially a nylon mallet which is pretty well indestructible. A good set of tools to tackle a fairly large in-the-round carving in sandstone or limestone would include (in addition to the carver's tools described in Chapter 1):

TOOLS LIST for 3D WORK

- 4cm (1½in.) pitcher (optional)

- Punch with 1.3cm (½in.) shaft

- 2.5cm (1in.) claw tool and bits

- 4.5cm (2in.) claw tool and bits (optional)

- 2cm (¾in.) tungsten carbide-tipped chisel

- Either a 3cm (1¼in.) or a 4cm (1½in.) tungsten carbide-tipped chisel

- Silicon carbide abrasive block 46 grade, for quick smoothing and removing tool marks

- For sharpening these larger tools, a 15cm (6in.) electric bench grinder is almost essential, with a 36 grit wheel for sharpening conventional steel tools on one side, and a 60 or 80 grit 'green' wheel for tungsten carbide tools on the other

THE FIRST EXERCISE –

MAKING A FLAT SURFACE

When I began masonry college, the first exercise was to make a flat surface on a stone block. We all thought, 'What's the point of that? We have stone saws to do that for us'. But there are two reasons why it is a useful exercise: firstly, it teaches control of the tools and processes, and secondly the methods can be applied to making non-flat surfaces which might be more interesting to sculptors. Trainee and apprentice masons and carvers have been doing this same exercise at least since the 12th century, when the great expansion of European church and cathedral building began. Before stone saws were invented in the early 20th century they worked every flat surface of every building stone in this way!

The stone shown above (1) is Stokes Ground, a limestone from near Bath in south-west England. It is honey-coloured and fairly coarse with visible oolites, and has been used extensively

1 The block with line marked on indicating level of stone to be removed.
2 Holding the pitcher in position against stone.
3 The bulk of stone removed.
4 Chasing the edges with a horizontal blade.

throughout southern England, particularly in Victorian churches. Stokes Ground stone is unusual in that it is mined rather than quarried, although other Bath stones are quarried. This block has an uneven top surface, perhaps because a large circular saw in the yard was aligned wrongly, and so it ended up on the pile for sale to impoverished stone carvers.

Begin by drawing the flat surface in the stone with a pencil. The next series of photos shows the traditional methods and tools used to arrive at a flat surface. The second photo (2) shows the pitcher being held against the stone, and the result of using it (3). You will see that the pitcher got very close to the pencil line, close

5 *Most of the remaining stone removed with a punch.*

7 *The surface worked with a chisel and hammer to remove claw marks.*

6 *Use a claw tool to clear away the next layer.*

8 *Finished surface smoothed down with silicon carbide blocks.*

enough so that most of the outline of the flat surface could be chased with a flat blade rather than an angled one. A 1cm (⅜in.) chisel was used (4).

Then use a punch to push lines through the stone from one side to the other, getting as close as you can to the depth of the new surface – most of the remaining stone is removed by the punch, and this is a key stage in the process. You need to practice the ability to 'see' the flat surface in the stone, and punch down to that surface, or as close to it as you can risk going (5).

Then use a claw tool to clear away the stone left between the punch lines and to get very close to the finished surface – use a straight edge to check that the surface is flat in all directions before continuing (6). Finally use a large chisel to take off the marks left by the claw. If your stone is soft you may be able to push the chisel across the stone by hand rather than using a hammer or mallet (7). Then take off all remaining tool marks with silicon carbide abrasive stones, finishing with an 80 grit stone (8).

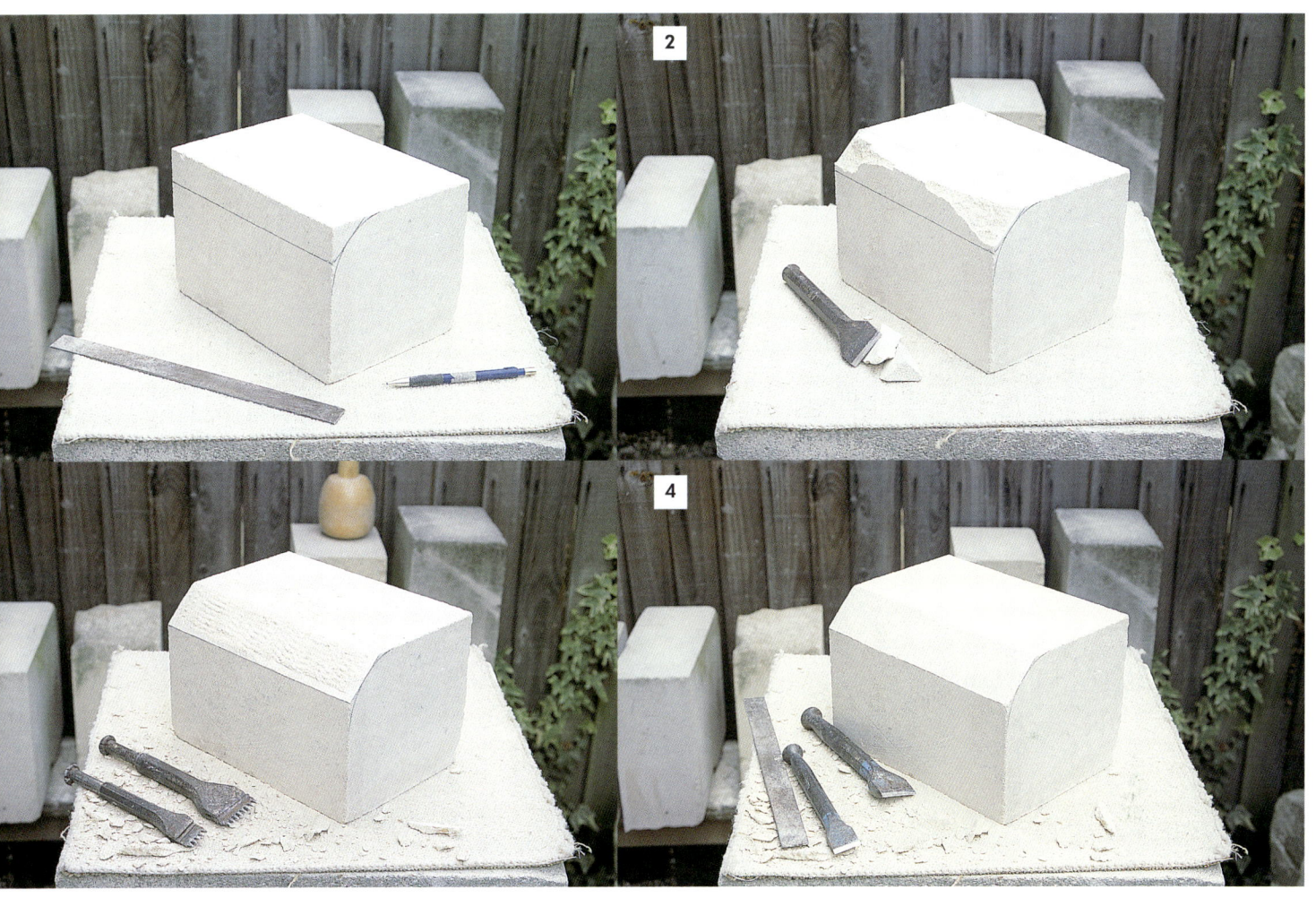

1 *Curve and chamfer marked on the stone.*
3 *Working the chamfer with a claw.*

2 *Using the pitcher.*
4 *Working the chamfer with a chisel.*

THE SECOND EXERCISE –

MAKING A CURVED EDGE

This exercise involves making a curve along an edge of the stone. Like cutting a flat surface, this method is a basic mason's skill, traditionally used to carve a simple architectural or decorative moulding onto a stone as well as a simple rounding as in this exercise. The method is to use repeated chamfers.

Draw a simple quarter-round curve on an edge of the stone and then draw a chamfer to touch the curve at its highest point. Where the chamfer intersects with the side and top faces of the stone, extend the lines to the full length of the stone, so that the line on the top of the stone and the line on the side is the same distance from the edge (1).

Work off this chamfer, first using a pitcher (2), then a claw tool (it is too small to use a punch) (3), then a chisel (4).

5 *Working the chamfer with abrasive blocks.*
7 *Secondary chamfers worked with a chisel and abrasive blocks.*

6 *Marking the secondary chamfers.*
8 *The curve finished with abrasive blocks.*

Finally, finish off with silicon carbide abrasive blocks (5). Then draw two more chamfers, above and below the first (6). These are shallower, and quicker to work off using just a wide chisel and a silicon carbide abrasive block (7). If you are working a hard stone you may need to cut a further series of four chamfers, but the curve on this stone could be finished with a silicon carbide abrasive stone (8).

These two exercises teach you a great deal about using and controlling the tools and judging surfaces, and, as we shall see in the next chapter, they can be applied to situations that are useful in making a free carving. The first exercise to make a flat surface can be applied to making a surface that is flat in one plane but curved in the other, and the repeated chamfers exercise can be applied to edges that are not straight to start with, or to make curves that vary along their length.

(Left) *A Bath stone carving (work in progress) by Robin Golden-Hann, for restoration of a Victorian Gothic Hotel (Rhinefield House Hotel) in the New Forest.*

(Right) *13th-century style head by Robin Golden-Hann. Carved from Chicksgrove Stone, a borderline limestone-sandstone. Part of the restoration work on Salisbury Cathedral (influenced by medieval carvings in the Chapter House). A carving at the junction of mouldings such as this is called a 'label stop'.*

As you carve three-dimensional pieces you will often use the sequence of tools described above, so it might be useful to summarise it. If you are starting from a block with sawn faces, draw the outline with a pencil and then use a pitcher to clear away the bulk of the stone above the outline. Then chase the outline; use a punch to push lines, or channels, across the stone — they should be as close as possible to the eventual depth of the carving. It's sometimes a good idea to pass the punch across the stone a second time, perpendicular to the first lines — this leaves less stone for the claw tool to remove. Then work off the stone left between the punch lines with a claw tool (perhaps using more than one pass — stone often plucks downwards at this stage, and you may go deeper than you intended). Then work off the claw marks with a wide chisel. Finish with a silicon carbide abrasive stone. This sequence is used several times during the next two projects.

PROJECT 3

AN IN-THE-ROUND CARVING

This chapter is about producing a free carving from a block of stone. Several 20th century artists such as Constantin Brancusi and Barbara Hepworth made sculptures that emphasised the mass and solidity of stone by using simple curves to produce abstract forms. The project detailed below is a simple piece designed to demonstrate some of the techniques and tools that might be useful when producing abstract sculpture in stone. You may prefer to use your own design, but if this is your first attempt at three-dimensional carving it is best not to make it too complex.

A BLOCK OF STONE

For three dimensional carving, the stone can, obviously, be any size, limited only by the original quarry block size, the size of the yard's stone saw, and your ability to move it. It should be at least 10cm (4in.) thick, to give a three-dimensional quality to the work.

As we noted in Chapter 2, large masonry yards sometimes keep damaged, broken or off-cut blocks to sell to carvers, like the piece of Bath stone used in the last chapter. These off-cut stones are cheap, or may even be given away, and are very useful for

Sculpture by John Valentine.

practising on or perhaps for making free sculptures the exact size of which isn't very important — obviously the carving has to fit the shape of the stone. But most of the stones produced by a masonry yard are sawn to a precise size and shape; those that have been sawn on all sides to exact measurements, ready for shaping by machine, mason or carver, are known in the trade as sawn six sides.

When choosing a piece (or deciding on the dimensions), bear in mind that sandstone and limestone can weigh up to 2.35 tonnes per cubic metre, or about 68kg (150lbs) per cubic foot, depending on density and water content. The stone used below was a sawn six block 30 x 30 x 13cm (about 12 x 12 x 5in.). Its volume was therefore 0.3 x 0.3 x 0.13 or about 0.012 cubic meters, and its weight 0.012 x 2.35 = 0.028 tonnes (about 28kg). In imperial measure this is a little over 60lbs. So, even this relatively small block needs two people (or mechanical assistance) to lift it onto the banker, although once it is there one person may be able to move it around without help.

The stone is Richmont Crème from Northern France. Richmont is a very close grained and quite soft limestone, which weathers well and is suitable for internal and external use, but it is damaged easily by impact, so is not used for garden furniture or flooring. Richmont Crème is sometimes used as a replacement for Caen stone, which is found in important buildings in Northern France (eg, Bayeux and St Etienne cathedrals) and in

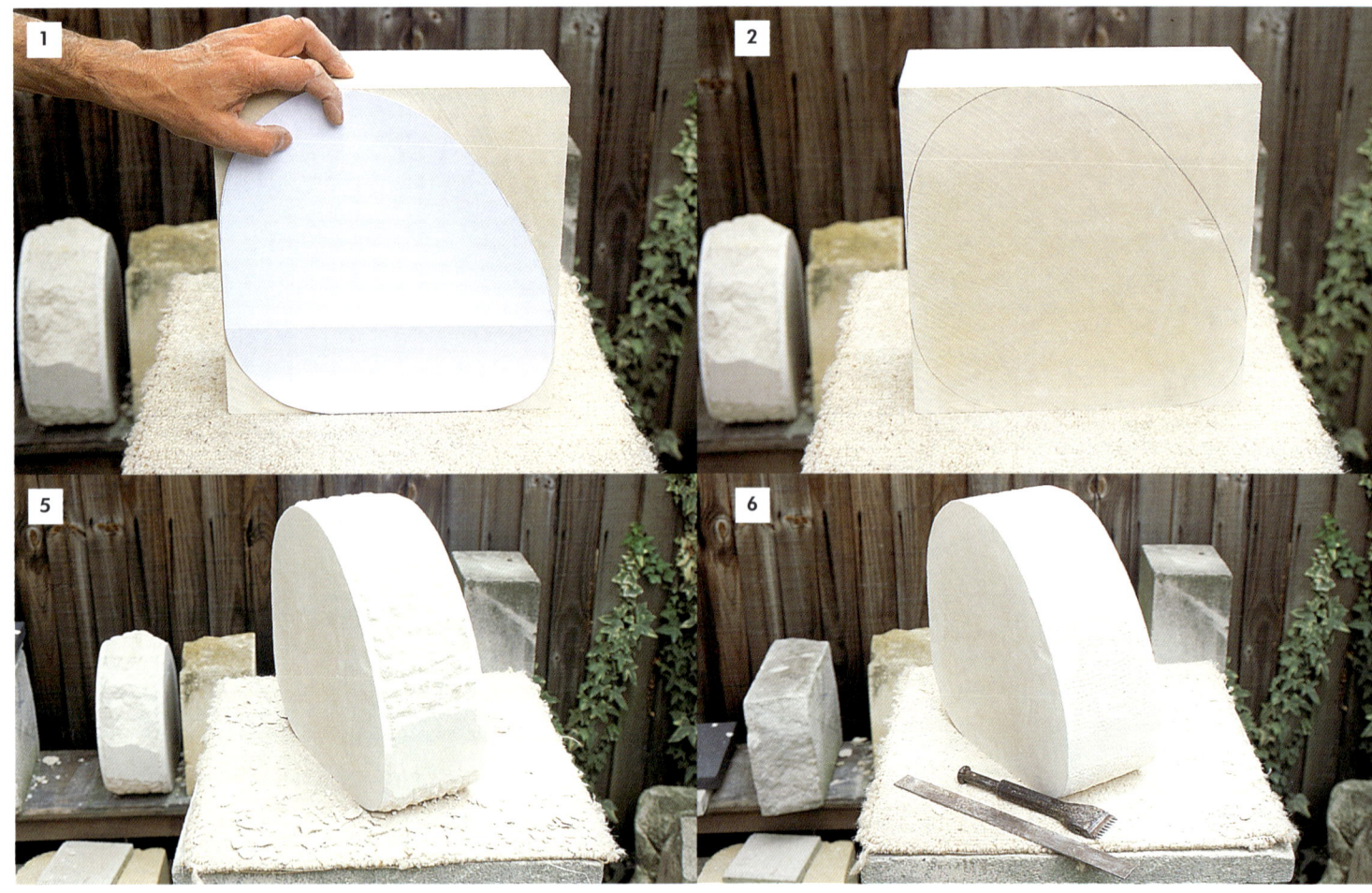

1 *Applying the template to the block.*
5 *Punching across the stone.*

2 *The outline of the form.*
6 *Using a claw tool.*

England (Canterbury cathedral, the Tower of London) dating from the 12th century, but is no longer available. Richmont Bleu has grey or blue markings that are particularly attractive when the stone is wet.

A cardboard template will make sure that the outline on the front and back of the stone is the same (1). The outline is drawn onto the face of the stone in pencil (2). Now is an ideal chance to use a pitcher, as it only works on sawn or flat surfaces; the photograph (3) shows how much stone can be removed using this tool, together with some of the pieces of stone removed. Making sure

you are wearing eye protection, work from both sides and, as always, don't try to do it all at once — just take off 2.5cm (1in.) or so with each blow of the hammer. Hold the leading edge of the pitcher flat against the side of the stone, handle extending towards you and held slightly downwards so that the direction of shock is slightly upwards. Remember that pitchers are very effective but not accurate, so don't try to pitch right down to the line — 3–5mm (⅛in.) away is about right.

Having used the pitcher to remove the bulk of the stone, now use a chisel (2cm/ ¾in. wide is ideal) to chase the outline

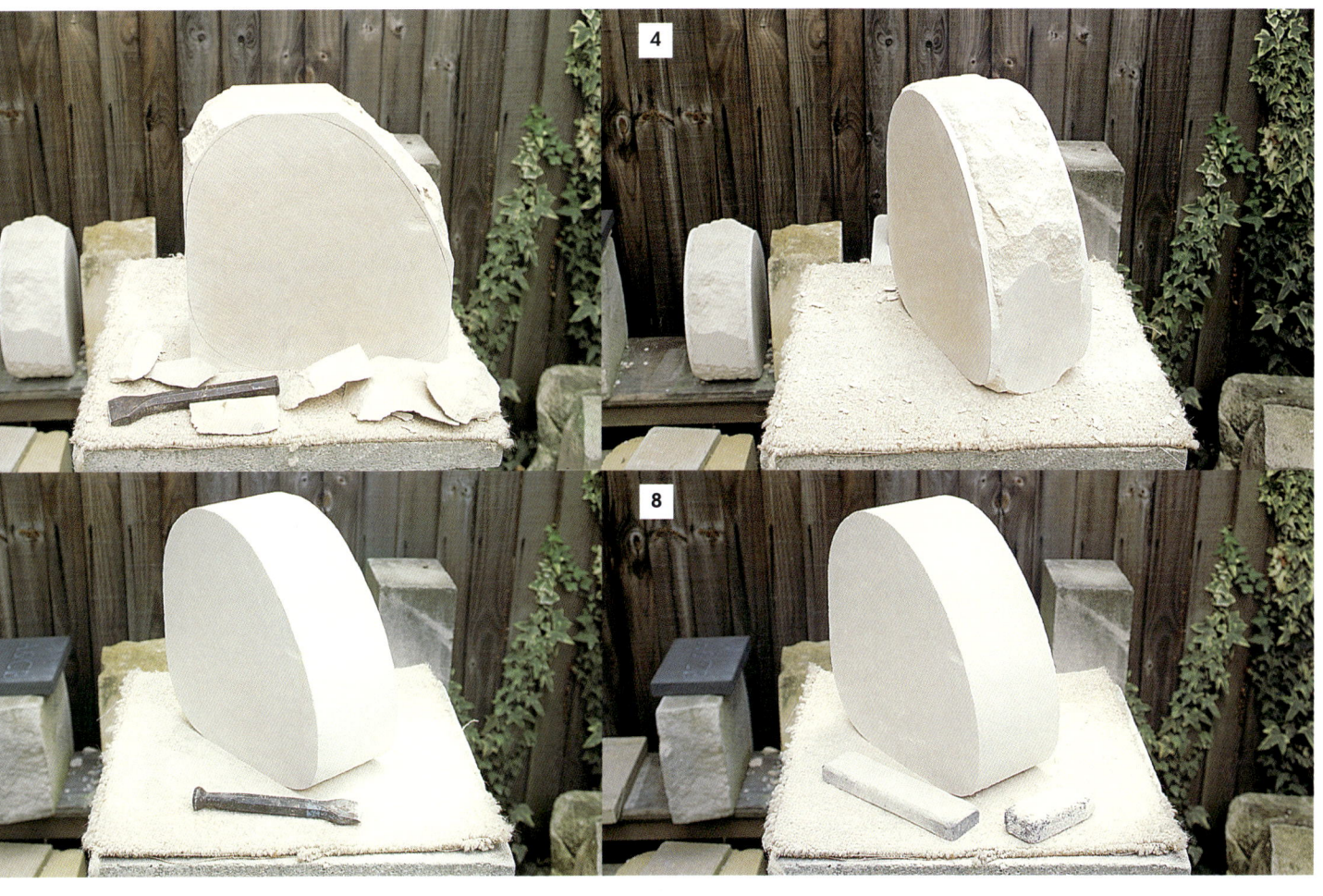

3 *After using the pitcher.*
7 *Using a flat chisel.*

4 *The outline marked with a flat chisel at edges on both sides.*
8 *Using abrasive blocks to finish off.*

on both sides of the stone. Where the pitcher did not get very close to the line you may need to cut an angled chase first, but you need to end up with accurately chiselled lines, perpendicular to the sides of the stone (4).

Now use the punch to cut channels across the stone, joining the two chases (5). The punch lines should be about 2cm (¾in.) apart, and quite a lot of stone will remain between the lines: sometimes it is useful to work the punch down the stone a second time, perpendicular to the first. Then work off the remaining stone with a claw tool, using a ruler or straight edge to make sure that the work is flat across the width of the stone at all points (6). Then work off the claw marks with a wide chisel – as noted in Chapter 5 you may be able to push the chisel by hand on soft stone (7) – before finishing with silicon carbide blocks (8).

What you have done is make a curve that is flat in one plane and curved in the other, using the same method and sequence of tools as used in the first exercise in the last chapter, which described making a flat surface. Now you will put curves on the front and back of the new flat plane by using repeated chamfers as described in the second exercise in the last chapter.

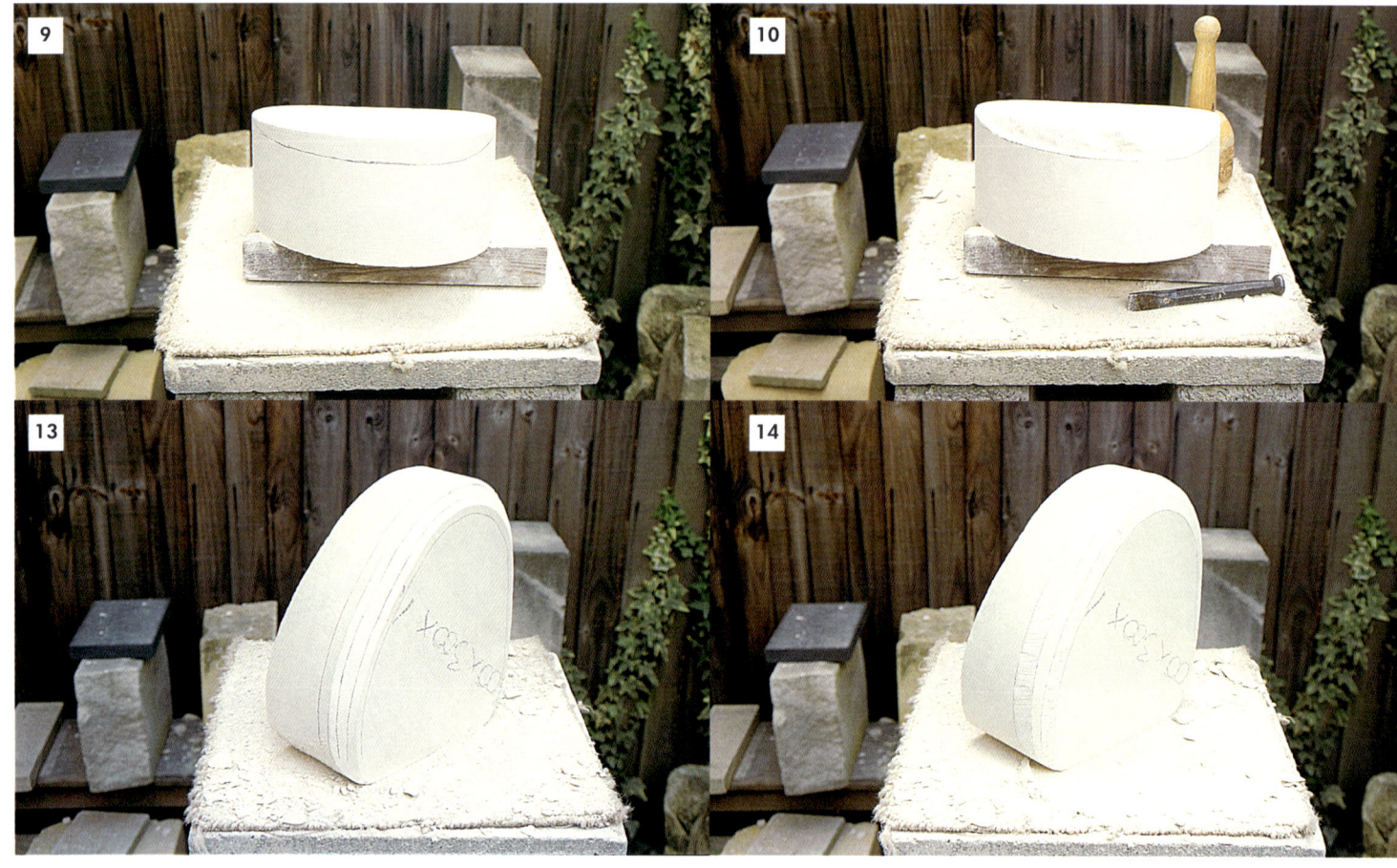

9 *Marking the slope on the front surface.*
13 *The first chamfer worked and the second chamfers marked.*

10 *Chasing the outline.*
14 *The second chamfers on the back surface worked.*

But before doing that, the finished carving would be more interesting if the front and back surfaces of the carving are not parallel — in other words, if there is a slope in the front surface. The method is now familiar, except that the pitcher is not used because there is no flat surface to apply it to. Mark the outline of the new surface with a pencil (9) and chase the line with a flat cut (10). Then work off the surface with punch, claw tool, flat chisel and silicon carbide abrasive stone (11).

Now work the curves on the front and back of the main curve by using the same method of repeated chamfers as shown above. The main difference is that the chamfers are made along an edge that is already curved. Mark the chamfer lines on the rear surface of the stone (12) (you can see the sawyer's mark on the back of the stone) and work off the chamfer with a claw and flat chisel. To make the pencil lines on the curved surface, try holding the pencil with your thumb, forefinger and middle finger, and using your fourth finger as a guide

11 *The new front slope worked smooth.*
12 *Marking the first chamfer on the back surface.*

15 *The same process on the front surface.*

16 *Working with the stone flat.*
17 *Both surfaces finished with abrasice blocks.*

against the stone run the pencil round the curve. With practice, this method is pretty accurate.

Then draw the secondary chamfer lines (13) (this time you will have to draw freehand) and work off these too (14). Use the same method on the front of the stone, but extend the curve further down the front surface (15). Work the stone flat on the banker if that is easier (16). Finally rub the curves with abrasive blocks (17).

18 *The shapes drawn on the stone.*

19 *The outlines chased with a small gouge.*
20 *The shapes worked with a point, curved claw tool and large gouge.*
21 *Finishing with small pieces of abrasive block.*
22 *The carving on a piece of shelly portland stone.*

Finally, a simple surface decoration is carved into the front of the piece, using gouges and a claw tool with a curved bit. Gouges are carving tools with a curved blade, very similar to woodcarver's gouges, and available in various sizes and shapes. They have firesharp blades. Alternatively, bull-nosed chisels are conventional flat chisels with the edges of the blade rounded off to a semicircular shape — if you have a bench grinder, you can make a bull-nosed chisel from a straight chisel that you accidentally dropped.

A simple pair of quotation-mark shapes is drawn onto the surface (18). This photograph shows the stone tilted backwards, and you may notice that the front bottom edge has been rounded off. Having carefully chased the outline with a gouge (19), the stone is cut away with a point (always remember to direct the point into the mass of stone) and then with a 2.5cm (1in.) claw tool with the bit rounded to a bull-nose shape on the bench grinder (20). The work is then smoothed with gouges or bull-nosed chisels (in soft stone they can be pushed by hand rather than struck with a hammer); the motif is repeated and the work is finished with small pieces of silicon carbide block (21). Finally, the carving was mounted on a simple plinth of very shelly white limestone, to give a subtle contrast to the piece (22).

PROJECT 4
A MORE FORMAL 3D CARVING

This project uses many of the same skills and techniques as those introduced in the last chapter, but in a more rigid context. It would not have mattered much for the project in the last chapter if the outline curve had been to a different line or if the shape of the quotation marks had been slightly different — ultimately the form of a free carving is for the carver or sculptor to decide on, according to their best artistic judgement. But there may be situations where someone else — a client or architect perhaps – has decided on the form of the piece and the size it should be. The commission may be a replacement for a damaged stone or have to match existing stonework.

The project worked in this chapter is an example of the end stone of a stone balustrade, known as a baluster die. A balustrade is an ornamental parapet to a balcony or terrace, made up of balusters (often teardrop-shaped, although this example is not) with a rail or coping on top. The balusters are circular on plan (that is, when seen from above) so usually they are turned on a stone lathe. But the die stones at each end are designed to look like half a baluster emerging from a block of stone, and so they have to be made by hand. They are an example of the kind of work that a stone carver working in a masonry yard would undertake.

This stone measured 43 x 18 x 15.5cm (about 17 x 7 x 6in.), and like the stone used in Chapter 5, it is Bath stone from the Stokes Ground mine. Templates are essential for accurate three-dimensional work. In Project 3 we used a cardboard template to make sure that the curves on the front and rear surfaces were the same, but it wouldn't have mattered much if we had drawn both curves freehand and if they had not turned out quite the same. In this project it does matter, however, because the baluster die stone has to match the other balusters in the balustrade.

(Opposite) *The Lion Gates, Hampton Court Palace, rear view. Designed by Sir Christopher Wren c.1700. Portland Stone.*
(Inset) *Detail of the panel showing the extent of undercutting and how little the stone has decayed in 300 years.*

1 *Applying the side template.*
5 *Chasing the outline on one side.*

2 *Applying the end template.*
6 *Working with a point.*

Mason's templates (sometimes called moulds) were traditionally made of sheet zinc, but are now usually cut from thick plastic sheet, as shown in the photographs below. When I was at masonry college we still used zinc, and the workshop technician used to collect all the bits of off-cut zinc, melt them down, cast the metal in a small cylindrical container, add a handle, and present each graduating student with a carving dummy which was the perfect weight and balance for letter cutting and fine relief work. Now carvers have to buy their own dummys, but plastic sheet is cheaper than sheet zinc, and is easier to draw on, cut and store.

3 *The outline shape on one side.*
7 *Working with a claw tool.*

4 *The outline shape on the top.*
8 *The first stage finished.*

Two templates are required for this project. One shows the profile, or side view, of the die stone, and the other shows the simple curve that applies to the top and bottom of the stone (1 and 2). Mark the profile template on both sides, and the smaller template on top and bottom — use a scriber, and then mark the scribed line with a sharp pencil (3 and 4). Work the profile along the sides of the stone in the usual way; chase the line (5) and then work the curved surfaces with a punch or point (6) followed by a claw tool (7) and finally with a flat chisel and silicon carbide abrasive stone (8), remembering to check that all parts of the work are flat across the width of the stone by using a ruler or straight edge.

9 *Working off the chamfers along the length of the stone.*
13 *The first stage in cutting in the narrow parts.*

10 *Working off the secondary chamfers.*
14 *The next stage.*

Now begin to work on the semi-circular curve, by the repeated chamfer method. Mark the ends of the first two chamfers on the top and bottom surfaces of the stone so that they touch the simple curves that you have already drawn. It is important that these marks result in an accurate semi-circular curve, so firstly they should be at 45 degrees to the sides and top of the stone, and secondly the width of the two chamfers should be the same, and the same as the surface that remains between them (9). Then mark the chamfer lines along the length of the stone — quite straightforward on the sides but

the lines on the top surface have to follow the existing curves. One way of doing this is to hold a straight edge vertically in position on the stone and hold the pencil against it, allowing the pencil to rise and fall as it follows the curve.

Then work off the chamfers in the usual way, with point, claw tool and flat chisel, but it is a bit more difficult this time because you soon have to cut across the profile curves you made earlier. So cut in from the both ends and then work off the middle part of the chamfers carefully, using a straight edge to make sure that the chamfers are the same

11 *The curve rubbed smooth.*
15 *A later stage.*

12 *The same stage from the side.*
16 *The reverse template.*

along the length of the stone.

Then mark the second set of chamfers, again making sure that the width of the chamfers and the stone remaining between them is the same (10). Then work off those chamfers (11) (the bottom line on these two photographs marks the end of the curve, not a chamfer line) and then rub in the curve along the length of the stone (12).

From here on, it becomes difficult to describe in words. You have to rely on experience and to trust your eye. Above all, take it slowly. Gently cut in the background to the half-baluster where it emerges from the stone block. At the same time begin to cut away the narrow parts of the half-baluster to meet the background (13). Feel your way into the stone until the shape begins to emerge (14 and 15).

Now make a small reverse template to guide you to the eventual shape of the curves: use your original profile template to provide the shape (16). Because the profile in this project is symmetrical, the same template can be applied to the top, bottom and central parts of the carving (17). If you were making a die stone for a traditional teardrop balustrade, the reverse template

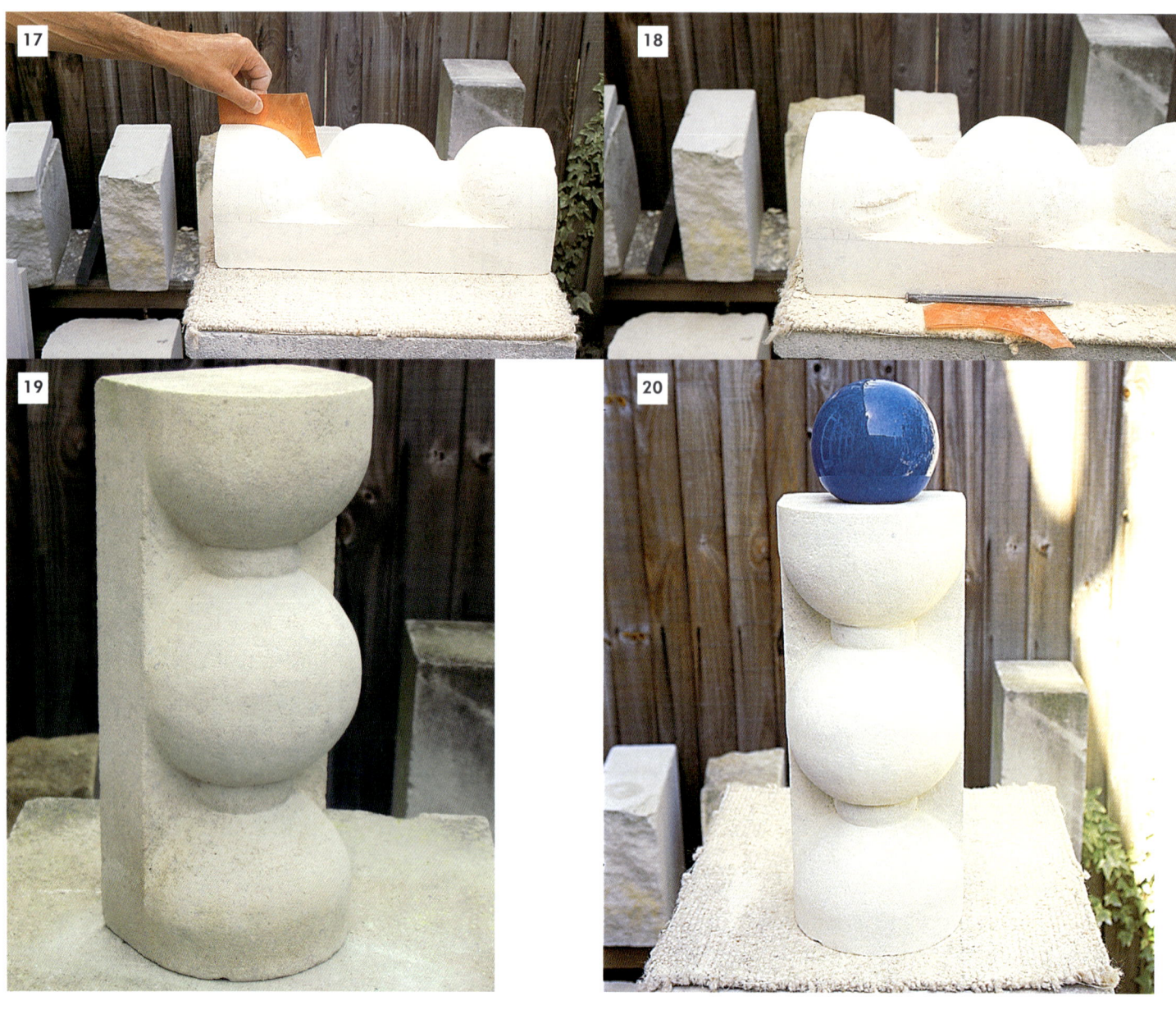

17 *Applying the reverse template.*
19 *The finished piece.*

18 *Approaching the finished profile.*
20 *Finished piece with ball on top.*

would be larger, to include the whole of the teardrop shape. Slowly work in all parts of the curves, guided by the reverse template, and gently carve in the profile to the waisted parts (18). Finally rub the carving to a smooth finish with abrasive blocks (19).

SOME EXAMPLES OF FORMAL CARVING

Above *A fine carved soffit above the doorway and* (left) *a carved panel to the doorway of Streatham Library, London, in Portland stone, 1912.*

Far Left *A decorative finial for Salisbury Cathedral carved by Robin Golden-Hann.*

CHAPTER 6

MENDING AND HANGING

If you have got this far without making a mistake, you must be very skilled, careful, or lucky; probably a combination. Mistakes are not always the carver's fault — you may come across a piece of shell or large grain of sand just where you are cutting an edge — but often mistakes occur because the carver tries to take off too much stone at one stroke, and plucks or flushes the stone. Either way, invisible, or almost invisible, repairs are possible, and this chapter describes some methods.

The first thing to make clear is that repairs are much easier on sedimentary stones (limestone and sandstone) than on marble or slate. The metamorphic stones often have deep and subtle colours and a highly polished finish that is very difficult to imitate, whereas sedimentary stones have a matt, slightly grainy surface that is easier to reproduce. It all depends on the size and shape of the repair, though if you miss-spell a name on an inscription (every carver's nightmare) you can do nothing except start again on a new piece of stone.

Dealing first with sedimentary stones, decide whether the mistake is large enough to warrant repairing at all. Small imperfections may not detract from the piece; a small flush on an edge may disappear if you round off the edges, as described in Project 1. However, having decided that a small repair is needed, here's how to do it.

Opposite *Some useful hand tools, including a depth gauge and dividers.*

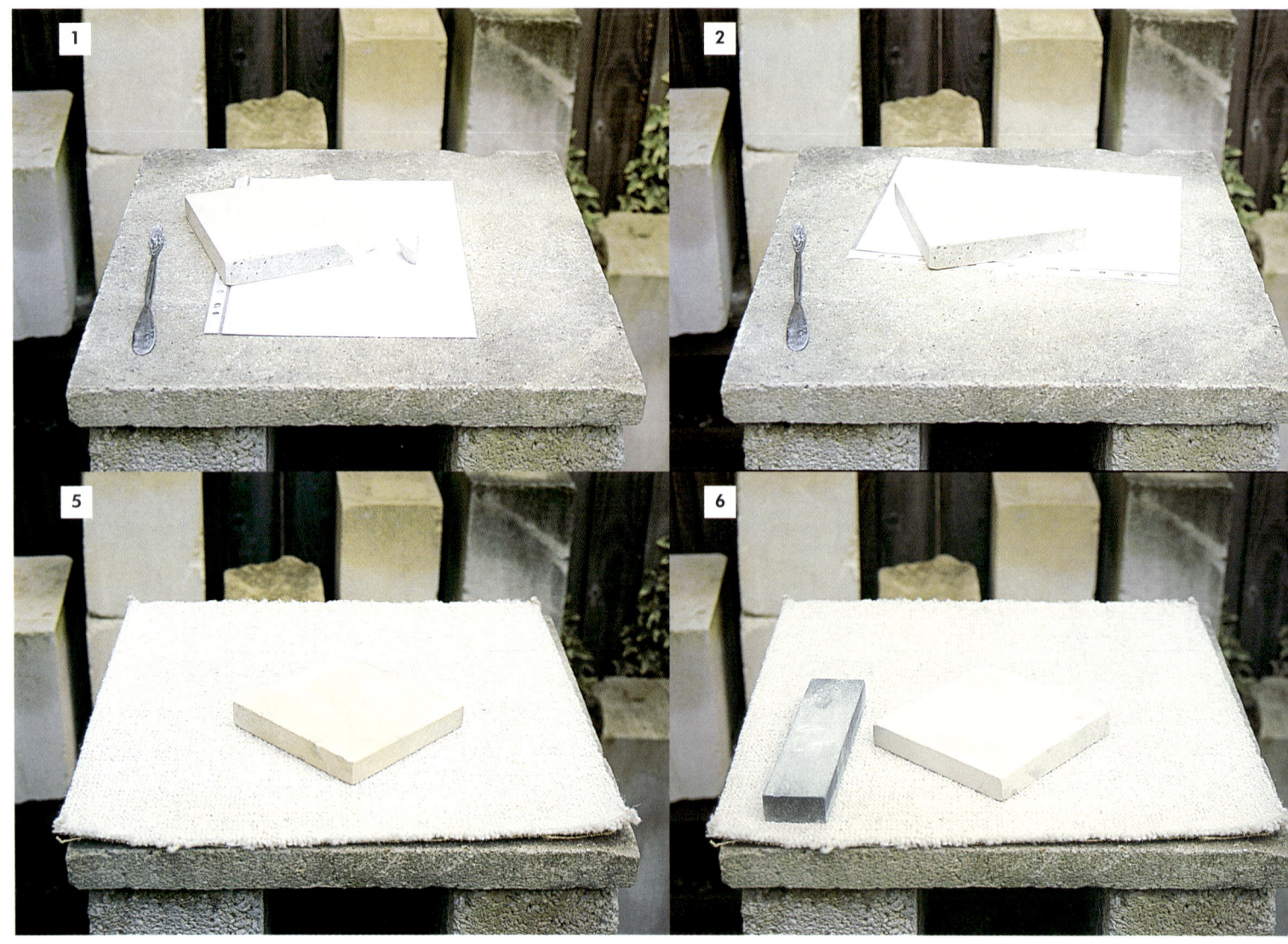

A BROKEN CORNER

When trying to re-attach broken corners, success depends on how clean the break is: if the pieces fit together closely, you will probably manage a good repair, even in marble and slate. Mason's epoxy resin is available from tool suppliers in white, a straw colour or transparent, and is the only material that is suitable for joining pieces of stone, certainly on a small scale.

This is a piece of Chinese sandstone from Guang Dong province with a broken corner (1). Successful repairs, especially on a small scale, depend on the surfaces being joined very closely, so that the repaired stone is perfectly smooth to the touch across the join. The repair must be clean and free of grains of stone; the photographs show one way of achieving this, by doing the work on a plastic document pocket with a piece of white card inside. The surface is flat, grains of stone

1 *The broken corner.*
2 *Corner glued with pure epoxy resin.*
3 *Gently clamp corner into position.*
4 *Hide any joins with resin.*
5 *Let the resin harden.*
6 *Rubbing down the repair with fine abrasive.*
7 *Finished repair.*

can be seen and brushed away, and the resin won't stick to the plastic.

Having brushed down the faces to be glued, make sure the pieces fit well before gluing, and brush them again. Join them with a minimum amount of resin mixed with hardener (2). Only a tiny quantity of hardener is needed — 2–4% by volume; once added the resin will begin to set in about 10 minutes, depending on the ambient temperature. While the resin is hardening, pressure can be applied by hand or by a clamp, but remember that the resin will tend to make the join a bit slippy (until it has set) so only apply enough pressure to keep the join in position (3). You may need to fill any small areas with more resin (4) and let the resin harden once more (5) before rubbing down the repair with a fine abrasive block (6). The finished repair is still visible, but not obvious (7).

1 *Flush to be filled at front of block. Epoxy resin and hardener with stone dust being mixed up at side.*

2 *Resin mixture applied to fill flush.*

FILLING A SMALL CHIP (OR FLUSH)

Masons and carvers usually use epoxy resin for filling, although cement-based fillers can also be used. As noted above the fillers are commonly available in clear, white or straw colours; cement is available in white or grey. Both produce durable repairs; the main advantage of the epoxy resin is that it sets to full strength very quickly, whereas cement-based repairs can take many hours or even a few days to harden. Another disadvantage of using cement is that it is often only available in large builder's sacks, so unless you have access to small amounts it may be impracticable to use it.

In this example the missing chip (called a flush by masons) on the front edge of the stone has been lost, and so must be made up with repair medium, in this case straw-coloured epoxy resin. Two important points about using epoxy resin: it must always be used in a well-ventilated area, and it must always be used on dry stone. It's a good idea to mix some crushed stone dust (from the same type of stone!) into the resin filler — this will add some unevenness to the very smooth surface of the resin. Collect a few chips from earlier work on the stone and grind them in a mortar and pestle, or drill a few small holes into the underneath of the stone and collect the dust. As before, make sure the work is done on a clean surface (1). Mix in the hardener (2–4%) and apply to the repair quickly (2). When hard (allow an hour or two to be sure) rub off the surplus with a 60 or 80 grit Carborundum stone.

The repair can still be seen (3) because of the texture as the colour and because the scratch marks in the resin from the rubbing stone are all in the same direction. Tap the repair gently with the corner of a Carborundum block so that the resin

3 *The repair rubbed down with silicon carbide block.*

4 *Repair after tapping the stone.*

surface reflects light more like the surrounding stone (4). The repair is now pretty well invisible, but another trade secret that is sometimes useful for larger or darker repairs involves an old toothbrush. Mix some fine stone dust with a little water and (to make it stick onto the stone) a tiny amount of PVA adhesive. Use the toothbrush to flick a fine spray of the stone dust and water mix at the repair and the close surrounding area; repeat two or three times. A hair dryer is useful to dry each application quickly and examine the effect. Don't use too much stone dust in the mix — it's better to use repeated applications — and don't use too much PVA as it tends to dry white. This technique takes practice but you can always rub it all off and try again; when you get it right it can produce a repair that will deceive the most practised eye.

All the above can be done with a cement-based repair. For light-coloured stones use white cement and add three or four times the volume of stone dust: for darker stones use grey cement and stone dust. Mix with water to form a paste and apply the repair to a damp (but not wet) area, and leave it overnight before rubbing down.

Repairs to marble and slate are much more difficult. Marble yards use clear (like water) resin, perhaps mixed with marble dust, and mechanically re-polish the larger repairs. Many repairs rely on the natural variation in stone colour to help disguise it. Sometimes coloured wax is melted and applied to very small flushes, but this is obviously not suitable where the marble or slate will be subject to heat or wear. Wax fillers and stoppers are used in various colours for very small flushes.

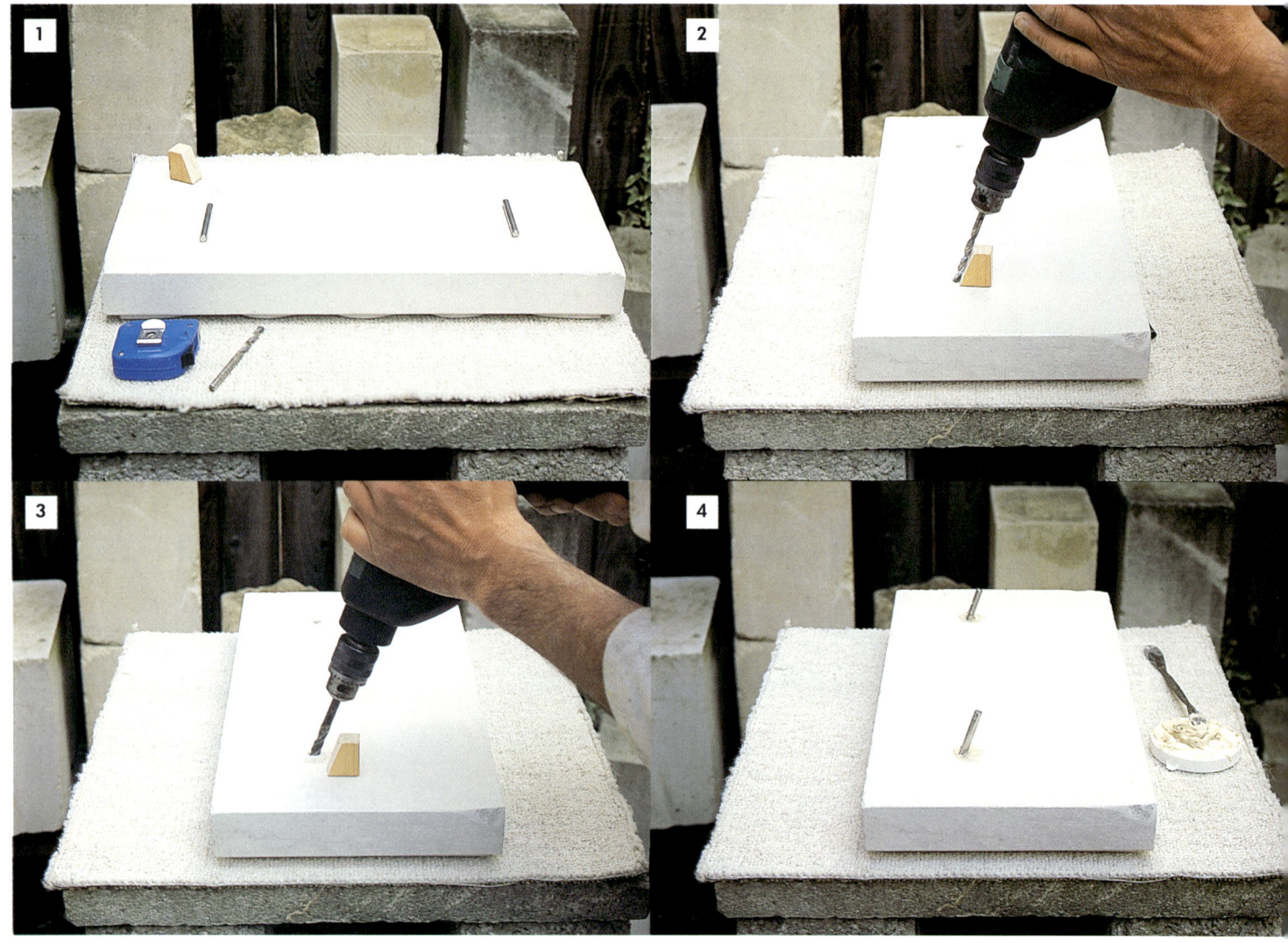

1 *Measuring the stone for final position of dowels, marking equal distances from edges.*
3 *Drilling same holes with an 8mm drill bit.*

2 *Drilling the dowel holes with a 6mm drill bit.*
4 *Setting the dowels into the stone with epoxy resin.*

HANGING

The next series of photographs demonstrate a simple hanging method, effective on external walls but also useful inside as long as the structure is strong enough. It involves stainless steel dowels fixed into the back of the stone at a slight angle from the horizontal — the dowels can be secured with either epoxy resin or cement. As before, the advantage of the resin is that it hardens very quickly but this time no stone dust is added to either medium: the resin is used straight from the tin and mixed with 2–4% hardener, and the cement (white or grey, it won't be seen) should be mixed with a little water to a thick mud consistency.

5 *The carving in position.*

The stone being hung is 5cm (2in.) thick and the dowels are 6cm long x 0.6cm diameter (2½ x ¼in. diameter). If the stone you are hanging is thinner than that, then the dowels should be proportionately shorter — the idea is to set a bit less than half the length into the stone, and a little more than half into the wall. The dowels can be cut with a hacksaw from a length of 6mm stainless steel rod, threaded or smooth, obtainable from a good building supplies outlet.

The position of the holes in the back of the stone must be carefully measured, and the holes marked out with hammer and chisel (1).

Use a home-made guide to help judge a consistent angle to drill the holes, mark the drill bits with a black felt-tipped pen about 3cm (1in.) from the point so you don't drill right through the stone, and drill the holes, first with a 0.6cm (¼in.) bit (2) and then with an 0.8cm (½in.) bit (3), this will make drilling easier, particularly in hard stone.

Clear out the stone dust from the holes, mix up the resin or the cement and fill the holes. Push the dowels in, clean off the cement or resin that is pushed back out, make sure the dowels are both at the correct angle, and leave them to set (4).

Using the same home-made guide, drill 0.8cm (¼in.) holes in the wall where the carving is to hang and guide the dowels into the holes. If you are drilling into brickwork, make sure the holes are in the bricks rather than the mortar (5).

There is no need to fix the dowels into the wall, unless you want to. If you are certain that the carving will hang permanently you can use a sand and cement pointing mortar to seal between the back edges of the carving and the wall.

The same technique can be used for fixing a carving into a recess, except that the dowels will need to be perpendicular to the back of the stone, and should also be fixed into the receiving holes with resin. The block with the carving is then fitted into the recess.

This is the reconstruction of a 14th-century style beast for Salisbury Cathedral by Robin Golden-Hann.

(Above) *Partial reconstruction of the beast using clay built on the remaining shape of the original stone as a model.*

(Top right) *Robin carving the new beast. The uncarved part of the block is then embedded in the wall. The stone can then be pointed (the edges around the join to the wall filled with stone dust and cement).*

(Right) *Finished beast installed in position on the north side of the nave.*

GALLERY

Column capital at Southwell Minster, about 1300.

(Left) *Cemetery memorial, London.*
(Above, top) Tenderness *by Bernard McGuigan. Forest of Dean Sandstone, 38 x 51 x 20cm (15 x 20 x 8in.).*
(Above, bottom) *Carving by Guy Levett.*

(Above) **Fragile** *by Robin Golden-Hann. Derbyshire limestone (known as Grange Mill) 70cm x 35cm (27½ x 14in.).*
(Far left) **Good Advice** *by Robin Golden-Hann. Nabresina (Italian) limestone and Cumbrian green slate, approx. 60cm (23½in.) high.*

(Above) **Be With Me** *by Bernard McGuigan. Pink alabaster, 30.5 x 30.5 x 15cm (12 x12 x 6in.).*

Panel carvings by Judith Tucker, from a series of four. They illustrate a high level of drawing and carving skill, and also show that you do not need fine-grained stones to produce fine detailing: as you can see from the photographs, they were made in a fairly coarse oolitic limestone.

Stone sculpture by John Valentine, used as a decorative garden feature.

Figure of a Woman *by Dame Barbara Hepworth. Sculpted from Corsehill stone, 1929–30.* Photo courtesy of Tate Images, © Bowness, Hepworth Estate.

Rock Face *by Dame Barbara Hepworth. Sculpted from Ancaster stone, 1973.* Photo courtesy of Tate Images, © Bowness, Hepworth Estate.

Pierced Form *by Dame Barbara Hepworth. Pentelicon marble, 1963–4.* Photo courtesy of Tate Images, © Bowness, Hepworth Estate.

Two Figures (Menhirs) *by Dame Barbara Hepworth. Slate, 1964.* Photo courtesy of Tate Images, © Bowness, Hepworth Estate.

GLOSSARY

ARRIS — The edge of a stone block.

BANKER — A workbench for carving or masonry work at a height suitable for use when standing, and positioned to be accessible from all sides.

BULL-NOSED CHISEL — A chisel with a flat blade and rounded corners.

CHAMFER — Formed when lines are drawn along both sides of the edge of a stone block, and the stone between the lines cut away to form an angled surface.

CHASE — A continuous line to dilineate an outline on a stone block, made with a small chisel with the blade held at approximately 45 degrees.

CLAW TOOL — A hand tool with a number of points instead of a blade. Some have replaceable bits.

DIAMOND SAWN — A stone surface cut with a diamond blade circular saw. The diamond blade often leaves saw marks on the stone

DUMMY — A light hammer with a cylindrical metal head used for letter carving and light relief work.

FINE RUBBED — A stone surface with saw or tool marks removed with grit stones.

FIRESHARP CHISEL — A chisel blade drawn out by a blacksmith in the traditional way.

FLUSH — A small shallow chip in a carving made in error, often on the edge or face of the stone.

FREESTONE — A stone that can be freely carved in any direction irrespective of the original bedding plane.

GOUGE — A chisel with a curved blade.

MALLET — A hammer made of wood or nylon with a rounded or cylindrical head.

MOULD — Template.

MOULDING — A decorative profile carved into the edge of a stone.

PITCHER — A tool applied perpendicular to the stone face, designed to remove large quantities of stone by sending shock waves through it.

PLUCKING — Unintentional removal of stone behind the chisel blade and below the intended surface.

POINT — A carving tool, like a chisel but with a pointed end.

POINTING — Filling the space between stone blocks with cement and stone dust mortar.

PUNCH — A larger and heavier version of the carver's point.

REBATE — Formed when lines are drawn along both sides of the edge of a stone block, and the stone between the lines cut away to form a groove or slot with sides perpendicular to the stone surfaces.

RELIEF CARVING — Carving intended to be seen from the front only.

RETURN — Where a moulding (or rebate, or chamfer) continues along a second edge of a stone block perpendicular to the first.

SAWN SIX — A cuboid stone block with all six sides sawn.

SCANT — Large thin sheets of (usually) granite or marble.

SCRIBER — A tool the same size and shape as a pencil, also used to mark a line. The sharp point creates a shallow depression in the surface of the stone.

SPARROWPECKING — An uneven background surface made by repeated light hammering.

STRAIGHT EDGE — A metal rule exactly straight along its length.

TUNGSTEN CARBIDE — A very hard compound used (among many other applications) in the tips of chisels, where it retains sharpness for long periods.

VENT — A hidden fault that causes failure and uncontrolled splitting in the stone when inadvertently opened by a carving tool in use.

RESOURCES

General

About Stone (US-based information about all aspects of stone, discussion forums, etc) (www.aboutstone.com)

Earth Science Education Unit, Keele University, UK (www.earthscienceeducation.com)

Natural Stone Directory (listings of companies involved in the UK stone industry) (www.naturalstonespecialist.com)

Suppliers of hand tools and equipment

UK
Alec Tiranti Ltd
3 Pipers Court
Berkshire Drive
Thatcham
Berkshire RG19 4ER
Tel: 0845 123 2100

(London shop)
27 Warren Street
London W1T 5NB
Tel: 020 7636 8565
(www.tiranti.co.uk)

Avery Knight and Bowlers Ltd
James Street West
Bath
Somerset BA1 2BT
Tel: 01225 425894
(www.averyknight.co.uk)

Crawshaws Ltd
3 Silverwing Industrial Park
Horatius Way
Croydon
Surrey CR0 4RU
Tel: 020 8686 7997
(www.crawshaws.co.uk)

Europe
Granidan
Ndr. Fasanvej 142
2000 Frederiksberg
Denmark
Tel: 0045 4484 1425
(www.granidan.com)

Guillet
BP 5, F-01150 Villebois
France
Tel: 04 74 37 69 00
(www.guillet-sa.fr)

Joseph et Fils
65, bd de Ménilmontant
75011 Paris
France
Tel: 01 47 00 92 29
(www.joseph-et-fils.fr)

Tabvlarasa
Viale Scalo S. Lorenzo 40
00185 Rome
Italy
Tel: 06 45420272
(www.tabvlarasa.com)

Talcus
Reithofer OEG
Am Ökopark 8
A-8230 Hartberg
Austria
Tel: 03332 66558 0
(www.talcus.at)

Canada
Micon Products
1325 Cartwright Street
Granville Island
Vancouver
BC V6H 3R7
Tel: 604 683 1285
(www.miconproducts.com)

Stoneman Distributors
Unit 1–79 Bessemer Rd
London
Ontario N6E 1P9
Tel: 519 668 3996
(www.stoneman.ca)

Terry's Stone Sculpture
Supply
2318A Lorne Avenue
Saskatoon
SK S7J 0S3
Tel: 306 978 2457
(www.terrysupply.com)

USA
Brad Oren Sculpture
Supply
800 Lone Oak Road
Eagan
MN 55121
Tel: 651 688 2000
(www.bradsculpture.com)

Montoya Sculpture and
Supply
502 Palm Street #21
West Palm Beach
FL 33401
Tel: 561 832 4401
(www.montoyasculpture.com)

Sculpture House
405 Skillman Road
PO Box 69
Skillman
NJ 08558
Tel: 609 466 2986
(www.sculpturehouse.com)

Stone Sculpture Supplies
P.O. Box 2124
Guerneville
CA 95446
Tel:707 869 1021
(www.stonesculpturesupplies.com)

Many of the above firms will supply tools on mail order. They will also either supply carving stone directly or advise on its procurement.

Some organisations that offer stone carving training

UK
City and Guilds of London Art School
(www.cityandguildsartschool.ac.uk)

Portland Sculpture and Quarry Trust
(www.learningstone.org)
Weymouth College
(www.weymouth.ac.uk)

USA
Southwest Stonecarving Association
(www.swstonecarving.org)

Stonecarvers Guild
(www.stonecarversguild.com)

The Stone Foundation
(www.stonefoundation.org)

INDEX

air tools 25
balustrade 71
banker 23, 27
basalt 12
bull nose chisel 68
Celtic knots patterns 39-46, 47
chalk 15
chamfer 34, 59, 60, 66, 74
chase 33, 41, 50, 57, 64, 72
claw tool 58, 59
chisels 28-29, 55-56
dimension stone 21
drawing 40, 49
epoxy resin 80-84

fine rubbed finish 23, 31
freestones 17
Golden-Hann, Robin 6, 7, 48, 52, 53, 61, 77, 89
gouges 68
granite 12, 17
headstones 49
Hepworth, Barbara 92, 93
honed finish 23, 31
igneous stone 12, 17
Levett, Guy 7, 88
McGuigan, Bernard 7, 88, 89
marble 17
mason 23 – 25

oolitic stone 14
pitcher 57, 59, 64
punch/point 36, 58, 64, 73
pointing 85, 86
quartz 12
scant 21, 23, 30
sedimentary stone 12, 17
silicon carbide 30, 46, 58, 60
slate 17, 49-53
Southwell Minster 8, 87
template 64, 72-75
travertine 15
Tucker, Judith 7, 90–91
Wessel, Fergus 7, 52, 53

Detail of the limestone carvings in the Chapter House at Southwell Minster.